GREAT AIR BATTLES

Also available in Piccolo True Adventures

GREAT SEA MYSTERIES
PIRATES AND BUCCANEERS
HIGHWAYMEN AND OUTLAWS
HAUNTED HOUSES

True Adventure Series

GREAT AIR BATTLES

An outline of war in the air with fourteen first-hand accounts by airmen who took part

ERIC WILLIAMS

Illustrations by Ley Kenyon

A Piccolo Original

PAN BOOKS LTD
LONDON

First published 1971 by Pan Books Ltd,
33 Tothill Street, London, S.W.1

ISBN 0 330 02827 8

Printed in Great Britain by
Cox and Wyman Ltd, London, Reading and Fakenham

CONTENTS

	Author's Note to Young Readers	vii
1	Gasbags	1
2	Early Birds	15
3	The Aces	25
4	*Blitzkreig* in Europe	42
5	The Battle of Britain	52
6	The Blitz	60
7	The High Seas Fleet	67
8	Kill The Admiral	75
9	The Master Bombers	83
10	*Festung Europa*	98
11	The Divine Wind	106

Author's Note to Young Readers

In this book you will read of some of the great air battles of the two World Wars. Where possible, the battle is described by an airman who fought in it, for I believe that only the man who took part can tell you truly how it was. I hope that after you have read the short passages quoted here you will read the airman's whole story. At the end of this book there is a list of titles, with the ones from which I have quoted starred.

From these first-hand accounts you will learn that while glorious things can happen in war, war is not glorious. Modern warfare means death, mutilation and misery for millions of people. You will learn that the airmen were often frightened. Few of them fought from a desire to kill. They fought to free their homeland from the invader, to prevent it from being invaded, from a youthful spirit of adventure – or, simply, because it was a job that had to be done.

The airmen called 'British' hailed from Australia, Canada, New Zealand, and South Africa, from what were then the Empire of India and the Colonies as well as from the British Isles.

Two of my younger brothers lost their lives in the RAF. Frank, a fighter pilot who had been awarded the Distinguished Flying Cross for gallantry in combat, died in a flying accident while his Spitfire squadron was 'on rest' in

Northern Ireland. Roy, a bomber pilot with me in 75 (New Zealand) Squadron, was shot down and killed over France while bombing the German U-boat pens at Lorient.

It is to Frank and Roy that I dedicate this book.

ERIC WILLIAMS

CHAPTER ONE

Gasbags

The first airman of all time had to fight to get into the air. For centuries inventors had been trying to design a craft that would take man off the ground. At last, by 1783, the brothers Joseph and Etienne Montgolfier of France had designed a hot-air balloon which, they confidently believed, was capable of lifting a man into the air and returning him safely to earth. Another Frenchman called Pilâtre de Rozier was determined to be the first man to fly. The King of France thought otherwise. He decreed that flying was too dangerous for honest men: criminals must be used to make the experiment. Rozier pleaded in vain until the Marquis d'Arlandes volunteered to accompany him, and the King yielded.

Their balloon was egg-shaped, 70 feet high and 46 feet in diameter, made of cotton fabric richly decorated with golden fleurs-de-lis and the signs of the Zodiac. Below a hole in the bottom hung an iron grating for the fire which was to heat the air inside the balloon and so cause it to rise. Round this grating and tied to the balloon with ropes was slung a basketwork platform for the crew. Rozier, who had already been aloft in a captive balloon, was the captain. The marquis fed the fire with straw and wool.

They 'rose with majesty' and sailed over Paris. Their chief concern was not to fall into the River Seine. Soon the fire set light to the cotton bag above them. They had ready a sponge and water, and dabbed at the burning fabric. Two of the basket's cords burned through but the remainder held. By feeding the fire to keep themselves airborne when over the river and the city, and by dowsing it when over a convenient field, they were able to bring their craft down safely. The marquis jumped from the basket while they were still a few feet off the ground, but Rozier waited and crawled from beneath the collapsed balloon. So ended the first free flight by man.

A Frenchwoman, Madame Thiblé, went up in a similar balloon a year later. A year after a Monsieur Blanchard and a Doctor Jeffries crossed the English Channel in a balloon which had been filled with hydrogen by the simple method of pouring sulphuric acid over iron filings beneath a hole in its bottom.

The Channel-crossing alerted the French generals and politicians. They realized that what they had judged 'an amusing toy' had military value. Soon two Balloon Corps were formed. The Austrians, who were then at war with the French, disliked the activities of the balloonists so much that they treated captured airmen as spies. Napoleon thought the Balloon Corps more trouble than they were worth, and disbanded them.

Half a century later, in the American Civil War, the Yankees sent up observers in balloons tied to the ground. From the air the observer was able to report the position of the Confederate forces.

During the 1870–71 Siege of Paris by the Prussians, the citizens used balloons to carry messages, and sometimes envoys, to the world outside.

The 'amusing toy' was useful, but it was difficult to control and as likely to land in enemy territory as in friendly. The addition of an internal combustion engine, a propeller and a rudder turned it into a more efficient weapon of war. These mechanized balloons were known as airships or dirigibles.

At the outbreak of the First World War in 1914 both the Germans and the British had the old type of captive observation balloon and the new type of dirigible. The British dirigible was called a Blimp and was used mainly by the Royal Naval Air Service to patrol the seas round Britain in search of enemy U-boats. The German dirigible was called a Zeppelin after its designer, Count von Zeppelin. Zeppelins were used as bombers.

Here, the commander of Zeppelin XII tells how he set out to raid London.

ERNST LEHMANN

On March 17th, 1915, the weather improved, and the radio repeated, 'Attack on London.' When I arrived at the hangar to give the order to 'Ready ship', I found my men at work. My officer reported; the chief engineer tested the engines; the helmsman checked the rudder controls and elevators; the gas valves and the water-ballast bags were in order; and the sailmaker used a paintbrush to retouch the camouflaging of the cover. Hydrogen hissed through the inflation tubes, the gasoline tanks were filled, and the capless bombs were hung in the release mechanism.

As soon as the airship was reported clear, I took my place in the control car while the watch officer remained outside to direct the launching. The sandbags, which weighed down the ship, were removed, and it rose from the wooden blocks on which the bumper bags rested. The ground crew grasped the handling lines, and at the command 'Airship march' they drew it out of the hangar. The watch officer was the last to swing aboard, and the man who substituted for him, or rather for his weight, jumped out. The ship was set against the wind and after releasing water, ballast was 'Weighed off'. Then with thundering motors it climbed up in wide curves to gain altitude and took course over Ostende to the North Sea.

The air was clear and calm and we searched in vain for a cloud behind which we could slip through the English coastal defence. Under us, on the shimmering sea, cruised enemy patrol boats; I prudently ordered lights out. The airship became a ghostly apparition. In the control car, the only light was on a dial of the machine telegraph. The two helmsmen stood like phantoms beside the wheel. In his narrow cubicle the radio operator sat with his headset over his ears, listening to the confusion of signals and voices whispering in the infinity of space. Under our keel the endweight of the antenna followed the airship like the spawn of a mother fish. The cold penetrated the control car through the floor and open windows. Despite two pairs of underwear, the leather jackets and helmets, we were cold. The Thermos bottle was passed around, and the coffee stimulated us.

To pass the time while waiting, van Gemmingen and I made an inspection tour. The watch officer and navigation officer remained in the control car with the helmsman. We climbed the smooth aluminium ladder leading to the walkway inside the ship. The head winds blew icily between the car and the body of the ship, pressing me to the ladder, and my gloved hands involuntarily clutched tighter round the rungs. It sometimes happened that a man was overcome by vertigo and slid off, falling 8,500 feet into the North Sea.

Even the walkway which extended through the entire ship was no promenade. In the darkness we made our way not so much with the aid of the self-illuminated plaques marking the route as by habit and instinct. On the narrow catwalk between the rigging and the tanks, we balanced ourselves as skilfully as if we were walking in broad daylight down a wide street. Like the rest I was wearing fur-lined shoes; and this thick footwear was not solely a protection from the cold. The hobnailed Army boot might have damaged the ship's metal frame, and shoes with rubber and straw soles were therefore regulation.

Near the gas cells, which threw shadows along the walkway like giant mushrooms in a prehistoric landscape, I heard a noise. In the light of my pocket torch I saw the sailmaker climbing about with a monkey-like dexterity. In his buttonless overalls he braced himself between two gas cells like a mountain climber in a rock chimney. He was searching for a leak in the cover. Brush and fabric glue were below him, close at hand if a bullet hole in the fabric had to be temporarily repaired. The sailmaker's duties involved great responsibility and were in themselves not without danger. Under certain circumstances he could be rendered unconscious by escaping gas almost before he knew it. Consequently, he always had an assistant or a comrade to attend him during his work.

On bombing raids I had no superfluous men aboard, and there was no such thing as relief after short watches, as in peacetime service. Thus the hammocks in the crew's quarters, which were slung between the girders, were empty now. There was only one man relieving himself of his inner feelings on the throne seat in the background. He jumped up in fright when he recognized me; but I smilingly motioned him back. The non-com who was the cook on board, reported in the darkness; I ordered him to give all hands a plate of soup from the aluminium pot on the fireless cooker – they could use something hot as long as the enemy was not making it hot for us. We did not carry much in the way of provisions, for they would have been superfluous – either we returned in twenty hours or we did not return at all. Our food was limited to bread, butter, ham, bacon, a few eggs, some preserves, a few bars of chocolate, and tea and coffee; we permitted ourselves a swallow of cognac only when we were back on land after a fulfilled mission.

Amidships, the narrow defile of the walkway widened out. Perpendicularly below me, the sea looked like lead. In the pale glimmer coming through the hatchway, I saw the bombs hanging in the release mechanism like rows of pears; besides explosive bombs weighing from 125 to 650 pounds, there were phosphorus bombs for igniting fires in the bombarded objectives. The safety catches were not yet off, but my bombing officer was already lying on his stomach, staring impatiently through the open trapdoor. He was a fine fellow and in peacetime would not hurt a fly but now he was eager to spill his murderous load overboard. We were at war, and war knows only severity towards the enemy, who repays in the same coin.

While Gemmingen discussed with the bomber officer the cooperation between him and the control car, I continued the inspection and descended to the aft engine car, which swayed under the airship like a celestial satellite. The car was enclosed and so crowded by the two 210-hp Maybach motors that the two mechanics could scarcely turn around. The noise of the motors drowned out every word, and the chief machinist simply raised his hand, which meant that everything was OK. The air in this nutshell was saturated with petrol fumes and exhaust gases. I almost choked, until I opened the outlet and let the icy air stream in. To exist for hours in this roaring devil's cauldron, where glowing heat and biting cold alternated, required a stone constitution and iron nerves. Yet it was as nothing compared to the demands made upon the mechanics when, during a battle with the enemy or the elements, the lives of the entire crew depended upon the repairing in mid-air of damage to the motor or propeller.

Proud of being permitted to lead such gallant men into the enemy's territory, I strolled through the marvellous structure that was our weapon and our home. In the darkness behind me, the stern, with its control and rudder fins, merged with the delicate filigree of girders. I passed the shaftway which led between two gas cells to the back of the airship, fifty feet up. There, on the platform beside his machine gun, hunched up in the winds created by the speed of the ship, the gunner acted as lookout and reported through the speaking tube the instant he sighted an enemy flyer. He was forbidden to shoot until he received the order to do so. For where the ship climbed, gas escaped upwards, and there was danger that a volley of gunfire might ignite the mixture of gas and air. Consequently, there could be shooting on the platform only when the ship was not releasing gas.

It was eleven o'clock when I returned to the control car. The ZXII had been cruising long enough, and now I set a direct course for England. The sharp coastline, with surf foaming against it, rose out of the dip of the horizon. And suddenly we had a queer feeling, as if our nerves were tightening in an almost joyous anticipation. Would we succeed in breaking through the chain of coastal batteries and remaining unobserved or at least undamaged? Strange that we could see so little of the mainland; it could not possibly have been that dark. The mystery was solved when we came closer, for suddenly we were in thick fog. The island was protecting itself from the flying invaders as it had protected itself from the invasions of enemy seamen centuries ago.

I brought the heavily laden ship as high as she would go. But at 10,000 feet the fog was just as thick. We cruised in all directions, constantly hoping to find the Thames, since the clouds are generally thinner over rivers. Finally I brought the ship down almost to the earth – in vain; the great metropolis was simply not to be found. We did arouse the furious fire of an anti-aircraft battery, which we were unable to find either. We had to owe it our reply.

In order not to waste the entire night in fruitless searching, we turned and steered for Calais. Much to our surprise, the weather conditions there were actually ideal for testing our observation basket under fire. The clouds were 4,000 feet high, and the air beneath them was clear as crystal. We could see the lights of Calais from miles away, and we prepared to attack. Gemmingen and I had a friendly quarrel because both of us wanted to get into the observation basket. Then Gemmingen pointed out that he was assigned to the airship as general staff officer and observer, whereas I, the commander, was obliged to remain in the control car. I had to admit that he was right.

Before we reached Calais, we throttled the motors so that they made the least possible noise while still permitting us to manoeuvre. The ship drove into the clouds, and Gemmingen was lowered 2,500 feet in the observation car. In the infinity of space he was suspended like a disembodied ghost. But as events were to prove, he was a dangerous ghost. When we arrived over the city, the observer hung 2,500 feet above it and had a clear view, whereas his tiny gondola was invisible from below. The garrison of the fort heard the sound of our motors, and all the light artillery began firing in the direction from which the noise seemed to come. But only once did a salvo come close enough for us to hear the crash of the exploding shells. When we leaned out of the car, we saw nothing but darkness and fog, but Gemmingen directed us by telephone and set the course by compass. Following his instructions, we circled over the fort for forty-five minutes, dropping small bombs here and larger ones there on the railway station, the warehouses, the munitions dumps, and other buildings. From time to time we noticed large oval spots on the clouds; they were the searchlights gleaming as through an outspread tablecloth.

Later we learned that a panic broke out in Calais not only as a result of the air attack, but because the airship remained invisible.

The commander of ZXII had made good use of a fortunately placed bank of cloud. Normally a Zeppelin was not an easy thing to hide either in the air or on the ground. Certainly it could carry a heavy load of bombs and, if unmolested, hover over its target while it dropped them. But as a target itself it was enormous, slow-moving, unwieldy and all too easy to set on fire.

Against the small, fast, manoeuvrable new flying machine – the aeroplane – the cumbersome Zeppelin stood no chance.

It was in a monoplane or single-winged aeroplane, a French Morane, that Flight Sub-Lieutenant R. A. Warneford of the RNAS brought down the first Zeppelin. He had set out from Dunkirk airfield in the dark early hours of a June morning in 1915 to bomb the Zeppelin sheds near the German-occupied town of

Beclem-Sainte-Agathe. Over Ghent he sighted, ahead and above him, the cigar-like shape of a Zeppelin on its way home from bombing England. Warneford decided that his own bombload would be better employed on this Zeppelin than on sheds which might be empty. He began to climb in order to get above his target. The Zeppelin's commander opened fire with all his guns in an effort to shoot Warneford down, or perhaps scare him off, before he could get into position to bomb. Warneford withdrew out of range and went on climbing. At 11,000 feet he was high enough. He turned in for the attack.

The Morane was a modified 'scout' or fighter machine and its bombs had to be dropped by hand. The 521-foot-long Zeppelin was so big that Warneford was sure that if he got close enough he could not miss. Flying along the length of the huge gasbag and 150 feet above it, he dropped his bombs. There was a terrific explosion which blew his Morane upside down. The Zeppelin, a flaming torch, sank slowly towards the earth.

Warneford had no time to watch it hit the ground because he himself was in trouble. The violence of the explosion had stopped his engine and he was unable to restart it is the usual way, by diving. He was behind the German lines, and after the dive had insufficient height to glide far enough to reach friendly territory. He descended and, in spite of the darkness made a perfect forced landing in a handy field.

Hastily he inspected his engine and found a fractured petrol pipe. He set to work to repair this before the Germans could capture him. At last it was done. There remained the problem of re-starting the engine and taking off.

On an airfield, one mechanic would stand ready to swing the propeller while another lay across the tail of

The Zeppelin, a flaming torch, sank slowly towards the earth

the machine to prevent this rising when the engine started. Two more waited to snatch wooden blocks from under the wheels when the machine was ready to move. The mechanic in front of the propeller would call, 'Switch off, petrol on, suck in!' The pilot checked that the ignition switch was off and that the fuel tap was on, and repeated the words loudly so that the mechanic could hear. The mechanic then turned the propeller slowly several times in order to fill the cylinder heads with petrol-and-air-mixture. Once he was satisfied that all cylinders had been primed he called, 'Contact!' The pilot switched on the ignition and repeated, 'Contact!' With one final heave on the propeller the mechanic ducked swiftly out of the way, the engine roared into life, the chocks were snatched clear, the man slid off the tail, the pilot taxied across the grass – and in a few seconds the machine was airborne. If the engine failed to start the whole drill began again.

Warneford had no one to help him, and with each passing moment capture seemed more certain. After several attempts he managed to swing the 'prop' and to scramble on board as his Morane began to move. He gave her full throttle and lurched through the darkness over the rough grass towards the far side of the field. Fortunately the Morane's take-off run was a short one, and he got away. He was back at Dunkirk in time for breakfast.

For shooting down Zepplin LZ 37 Flight Sub-Lieutenant Warneford was awarded the Victoria Cross, the highest British military honour. A few days later he was killed in a flying accident.

After this first victory Zeppelin after Zeppelin was brought down, some by the increasingly accurate anti-aircraft fire from the ground, some by airmen.

The anti-aircraft fire could be as great a hazard to friend as to foe. Hunting Zeppelins over London on a night in October 1916, 2nd Lieutenant W. J. Tempest of the Royal Flying Corps sighted one caught in a cone of searchlights fifteen miles away and had to make for her through the London barrage – 'a very inferno of bursting shells'. The petrol was fed to his engine by an automatic pump. Before he could engage the enemy, when he was flying at a height of 15,000 feet, the pump broke down. In his report he describes what happened:

'I had to use my hand pump. This exercise at so high an altitude was very exhausting, besides occupying an arm and thus giving me one hand less to operate with when I commenced to fire.' By the time he reached his objective, the Zeppelin had let go her bombs and was climbing to gain safe height for her flight home. He knew that there was no time to be lost or she would be too high for him to follow. 'I accordingly gave a tremendous pump at my petrol tank and dived straight for her, firing a burst straight into her as I came. I let her have another burst as I passed under her and then banked my machine over, sat under her tail, and flying along underneath her pumped lead into her for all I was worth. As I was firing I noticed her begin to go red inside like an enormous Chinese lantern. She shot up about 200 feet, paused, and came roaring down straight on to me before I had time to get out of the way. I nose-dived for all I was worth, with the Zeppelin tearing after me. I put my machine into a spin and just managed to corkscrew out of the way as she shot past me roaring like a furnace. She struck the ground in a shower of sparks. I then proceeded to fire off dozens of green Very lights in the exuberance of my feelings.'

The next morning it was discovered, from the wreck of

the Zeppelin near Potters Bar, that the dead commander was *Kapitanleutnant* Heinrich Mathy, who had been one of the most persistent and successful raiders on London.

In spite of such losses the German High Command continued to send the occasional Zeppelin to bomb England, and the British Admiralty used their 45-mph Blimps to escort convoys and hunt U-boats; but before the end of the First World War both sides realized that as a weapon of war the dirigible or airship had been outdated by the heavier-than-air machine.

The only gasbags used in the Second World War were captive barrage balloons. Forests of these floated in the air over cities and other important ground targets, as well as shipping. The balloons were not manned but their steel cables were a protection against low-level attacks by hostile aircraft.

CHAPTER TWO

Early Birds

The aeroplane is an invention of the twentieth century. Its design developed almost simultaneously in countries thousands of miles apart. The American brothers Orville and Wilbur Wright made the first officially recorded flight in a biplane in 1903 – at a height of ten feet above the ground. At about that time a New Zealand farmer, Richard William Pearse, flew round one of his fields in a contraption he had fashioned himself of bamboo, canvas, baling wire and beaten-out tin cans.

In 1908 an Englishman, Dr Alliott Verdon-Rowe, flew a British-built machine over Brooklands motor-car race track; and by 1912 the French had so improved the design that the aviator Pégoud was able to loop the loop.

The British Government was expecting war with Germany. The Royal Aircraft Establishment at Farnborough, which had hitherto produced only balloons, now set to work to try to produce better aeroplanes than the Germans had.

By 1914, when the First World War broke out, the British and their French Allies had lighter-than-air airships and observation balloons, and heavier-than-air aeroplanes and seaplanes. They also had a nucleus of trained aviators, and an ever-growing queue of volunteers as eager to fly as to fight.

So, too, did the enemy.

In the early days flying training did not take long. The recruit went up with an instructor in a dual-control machine which took off from the ground at forty miles per hour and had a maximum speed only five or six miles faster.

The instructor showed him the joystick, the rudderbar and throttle. When he pulled the joystick towards him the aeroplane pointed upwards, when he pushed it away she dived, when he moved it sideways she tilted or banked that way. With the rudderbar he steered her to port or starboard, and with the throttle he controlled the engine speed.

After, sometimes, only a couple of hours' instruction the pupil went solo. If he returned to the field with his machine intact he was reckoned to be good pilot material. With only a few more hours' flying to his credit he was given his wings and sent off to fight.

Now he had to learn to fly more up-to-date machines – monoplanes, biplanes or triplanes – some of them with speeds as high as 100 mph. He had to learn to fly them so well that he did not think about flying, so that when he met the enemy in the air he would do the right thing instinctively. Where he had learned to fly straight and level, he now had to learn to corkscrew and weave and zoom and dive in an effort to confuse the gunners on the ground.

Mere flying skill was not enough. The airman also needed luck. His engine could fail, a wing could fall off his flimsy machine in a dive, his guns could (and often did) jam at the wrong moment, a stray rifle-shot from the ground could hit him or his machine, he could be caught out in a thunderstorm or lost in low cloud or fog, he could run out of petrol over the enemy lines.

In the First World War the battling armies did not move far. They fought for the possession of lines of trenches in Flanders (North-eastern France and Belgium). There the usual wind is from the west. This favoured the German airman – the Hun, Boche or Jerry as the Allies called the enemy – by carrying him safely home in a glide even when his machine was damaged. An Allied airman often found himself, at the end of a patrol, behind the German lines. If forced down he was taken prisoner.

Luckily the early aeroplanes, if not too badly damaged, could with skilful handling glide down and land safely on any small clear space. The pilot could not bale out. Although the Germans were issued with parachutes during the last months of the First World War, the only Allied airmen who had parachutes then were the balloon observers.

At first military aeroplanes were used more for reconnaissance and artillery spotting – helping to direct the heavy guns on to their target – than as fighters or bombers. This Army liaison work was done by aeroplanes manned by a crew of two, a pilot and an observer. Cecil Lewis, who gained his wings and the King's Commission in the RFC at the age of seventeen, describes his first operation. He was flying a 72-mph BE 2c biplane developed at Farnborough.

CECIL LEWIS

The surveying of the German line was difficult from the ground. You couldn't very well walk about with a theodolite and a chain in full view of the enemy, so the making of maps was largely a matter of aerial photography. In the spring of 1916, with the big offensive on the Somme preparing, the accuracy of these maps was of the greatest importance. So our job that day was to go over the front line at 7,500 feet and fly all along the enemy second-line trenches from Montauban, round the Fricourt salient and up to Boisselle, photographing as we went.

If there was ever an aeroplane unsuited for active service, it was the BE 2c. The pilot sat slightly aft of the main planes and had a fair view above and below, except where the lower main plane obscured the ground forward; but the observer, who sat in front of him, could see practically nothing, for he was wedged under the small centre section, with a plane above, another below, and bracing wires all round He carried a gun for defence purposes; but he could not fire it forwards, because of the propeller. Backwards, the centre-section struts, wires, and the tailplane cramped his style.

The observer could not operate the camera from his seat because of the plane directly below him, so it was clamped on outside the fuselage, beside the pilot; a big, square, shiny mahogany box with a handle on top to change the plates (yes, plates!). To make an exposure you pulled a ring on the end of a cord. To sight it, you leaned over the side and looked through a ball and cross-wire finder. The pilot, then, had to fly the machine with his left hand, get over the spot on the ground he wanted to photograph – not so easy as you might think – put his arm out into the 70-mph wind, and push the camera handle back and forwards to change the plates, pulling the string between each operation. Photography in 1916 was somewhat amateurish.

So I set out on that sunny afternoon, with a sergeant-gunner in the front seat, and climbed up towards the

lines. As I approached them, I made out the place where
we were to start on the ground, comparing it with the
map. Two miles the other side of the front line didn't
look far on paper; but it seemed a devil of a way when
you had to fly vertically over the spot. The sergeant knelt
on his seat, placed a drum on the Lewis gun, and faced
round over the tail, keeping a wary eye open for Fokkers.
But the sky was deserted, the line quiet. Jerry was having
a day off. I turned the machine round to start on my
steady course above the trenches, when two little puffs of
grey smoke appeared a hundred feet below us, on the left.
The sergeant pointed and smiled: 'Archie!'* Then three
others appeared closer, at our own height. It was funny
the way the balls of smoke appeared magically in the
empty air, and were followed a moment later by a little
flat report. If they didn't range us any better than that
they were not very formidable, I thought, and began to
operate the camera handle

There are times in life when the faculties seem to be
keyed up to superhuman tension. You are not necessarily
doing anything but you are in a state of awareness, of
tremendous alertness, ready to act instantaneously should
the need arise. Outwardly, that day, I was calm, busy
keeping the trenches in the camera sight, manipulating
the handle, pulling the string; but inside my heart was
pounding and my nerves straining, waiting for something, I did not know what, to happen. It was my first
job. I was under fire for the first time. Would Archie get
the range? Would the dreaded Fokker appear? Would the
engine give out? It was the fear of the unforeseen, the
inescapable, the imminent hand of death which might,

* *Archie* – slang for anti-aircraft fire, taken from a popular music hall
song *Archibald! Certainly Not!* It was called *ack-ack* (British) or *flak*
(German) in the Second World War.

from moment to moment, be ruthlessly laid upon me.

I went on pulling the string and changing the plates when, out of the corner of my eye, I saw something black ahead of the machine. I looked up quickly; there was nothing there. I blinked. Surely, if my eyes were worth anything, there had been something . . . Yes! There it was again! This time I focused. It was a howitzer shell, one of our own shells, slowing up as it reached the top of its trajectory, turning slowly over and over, like an ambling porpoise, and then plunging down to burst. Guns fire shells in a flat trajectory; howitzers fling them high, like a lobbed tennis ball. It follows that, if you happen to be at the right height, you catch the shell just as if hovers at its peak point. If you are quick-sighted you can then follow its course down to the ground. I watched the thing fascinated. Damn it, they weren't missing the machine by much, I thought; but I was left little time to consider it, for suddenly there was a sharp tearing sound like a close crack of thunder, and the machine was flung upwards by the force of the explosion of an Archie burst right underneath us. A split second later, and it would have been a direct hit. A long tear appeared in the fabric of the plane where a piece of shrapnel had gone through. There was a momentary smell of acrid smoke. 'S-turns!' shouted the sergeant. 'They've ranged us!' I flung the machine over and flew west, then turned again, and again, and again . . . The Archie bursts were distant now. We had thrown them off.

'How many more?' shouted the sergeant, with a jerk of his head to the camera box.

'Two.'

Flying on a steady course is the surest way to get caught by Archie, and we had been, right enough. If we were quick we might snatch the other two photos and get away before he ranged us again. I turned back over the spot, pulled the string and flew to make the last exposure, when the sergeant suddenly stiffened in his seat, cocked his gun, and pointed: 'Fokker!'

I turned in my seat and saw the thin line of the monoplane coming down on our tail. He had seen the Archie bursts, no doubt, had a look round to see if we were escorted, and, finding it all clear, was coming down for a sitter.

I got the last photo as he opened fire. The distant chatter of his gun was hardly audible above the engine roar. It didn't seem to be directed at us. He was, I know now, an inexperienced pilot, he should have held his fire. We replied with a chatter that deafened me, the muzzle of the Lewis gun right above my head. The Fokker hesitated, pulled over for a moment, and then turned at us again. The sergeant pulled his trigger. Nothing happened. 'Jammed! Jammed!' he shouted. He pulled frantically at the gun, while the stuttering Fokker came up. I put the old 2c right over to turn under him. As I did so, there was a sharp crack, and the little windscreen a foot in front of my face showed a hole with a spider's web in the glass round it.

It was Triplex: no splinters; but another foot behind would have put that bullet through my head – which was not Triplex. A narrow shave. Instinctively I stood the machine on its head and dived for home. At that moment, as if to cap all, the engine set up a fearful racket. The whole machine felt as if it would fall to pieces.

'Switch off! Switch off!' yelled the sergeant. 'The engine's hit.'

I obeyed, still diving, turning sharply as I did so to offer a more difficult target to the Fokker. But, luckily for us, he decided not to pursue. In those days the Huns did not adventure much beyond their own side of the lines, and now we were back over ours.

We saw him zoom away again. He had us at his mercy, had he known. There was a moment of wonderful relief.

The Fokker turned at us again

We laughed. It had all happened in much less time than it takes to tell, and we were still alive, safe!

'Make for the advance landing ground,' shouted the sergeant. He was furious with the gun jamming, jumpy at our narrow shave, and, anyway, didn't relish his job with inexperienced pilots like me, just out from home.

I spotted the advance landing ground – thank heaven I had been down on it previously – and circled to make my landing. It would have been a fine thing, I thought, if that had happened a few miles farther over and I had been forced down in Hunland on my first patrol. I skimmed over the telegraph poles, got down without mishap, and jumped out to examine the machine.

The sergeant was apostrophizing the gun. 'These bloody double drums!' he said. 'Always jamming! He had us sitting, God damn it!'

I pulled over the prop. There was a hollow rattle from the inside. Something serious, a big end gone, or a smashed connecting-rod, probably. Anyway, they would have to send out another engine . . . But we were down! Here was the ground under my feet; the sky above, serene, impersonal; the machine solid beneath my touch, swaying slightly in the wind. All that remained to bear witness of our escape was the rattle of the engine, the tear in the plane, the smashed windscreen, and the tiny perforations of the bullet holes in the body, two down behind my seat, more in the tail.

Preventing reconnaissance and artillery spotting by the other side became more and more important. Planes were sent up to shoot down observation balloons. This was not so simple as it sounds. These new gasbags (filled with hydrogen) were attached by steel cables to winches mounted on lorries. An observer spent the daylight hours in a basket slung beneath the balloon. He was armed with a rifle; but his chief defence was from the ground, where the gunners knew the exact height at which he floated and therefore had the range of the attacking aeroplane. An American, Frank Luke, made history by shooting down fourteen balloons and five planes in fourteen days.

New military uses were found for the aeroplane. It landed spies behind the enemy lines. It dropped bombs on railway junctions, ships and troop concentrations. The more it was used offensively the more necessary it became to shoot it down. 'Archie' was not enough. Squadrons were formed of skilled aggressive young men – the first fighter pilots. Soon these were not only shooting down balloons and reconnaissance planes but were also engaging in aerial battles with enemy fighters.

CHAPTER THREE

The Aces

The weapons of the early warplanes were primitive. Revolvers, rifles, even shotguns were carried by the observers. Heavy weights suspended on wire were dangled in the hope of entangling the enemy's propeller. Grenades were lowered on string and detonated from above. Small incendiary bombs and showers of pointed steel darts, like lead pencils, were dropped on the enemy plane.

Later, movable machine guns were mounted on brackets in the observers' cockpits. These had a limited field of fire if the gunner was not to hit his own aeroplane – or his pilot. It was not easy for him to transfer the heavy gun from one side of the cockpit to the other when the machine was flying high and fast and his hands were frozen or clumsy in gloves.

Later still, guns were fixed above the wings, to fire forwards over the arc of the propeller, so that the pilot, too, could fire.

The pilots were not satisfied. They wanted to fire *through* the arc of the propeller. A Frenchman, Roland Garros, who had become famous as an aviator before the war, added steel plates to protect the wooden blades of his Morane monoplane. It was a simple device but it worked. Then the Allies had bad luck. Garros made a forced landing behind the German lines and was captured before he could set fire to his Morane. The Germans seized on the new idea and asked the aeroplane designer, Anton Fokker, to improve on it. Within three days Fokker had invented a synchronizing gear which enabled the machine gun to fire through the arc of the propeller without hitting the blades. With a push-button gun trigger fitted to the joystick, the pilot could fire by merely moving his thumb.

It was no longer necessary for a fighter to carry an observer as gunner. The pilot could aim his whole machine at the target and do the fighting himself.

When the Allies captured a new Fokker aeroplane intact, they in their turn seized on their enemy's invention. Both sides were equal again in their firepower. Manoeuvrability of the aeroplane itself, and the pilot's skill in using it, were all-important.

The first fighter pilots had no textbooks to learn from and often no expert to teach them. They taught themselves and each other. On the ground they spent their leisure hours discussing tactics. In the air they pushed their machines to the limit, practising the aerobatics – the spins, stall turns, vertical banks, loops, barrel rolls and rolls off the top – which would help them dodge the enemy and put themselves in the best position for attack.

A German, Max Immelmann, invented the 'Immelmann turn'. He would dive on his opponent, fire, zoom upwards and peel off into another dive to bring him back upon his enemy but from the opposite direction. Until then, Immelmann had been renowned only for the number of aeroplanes he had crashed while training!

Immelmann was expert too at flying between the sun and an opponent who, dazzled by the light, could not see his attacker until too late. (In the Second World War one of the first things we were taught was: *Beware of the Hun in the sun. Beware of the Goon in the moon*.) In defence against this tactic, fighters began to fly in pairs, one behind and slightly above the other in order to protect his leader from attack.

Sometimes whole squadrons flew in close formation. Strangely, this proved to be less, not more, safe. Each pilot assumed that the others were keeping a good all-round lookout. Lulled into a sense of security in numbers, a squadron could be surprised and scattered by only two of the enemy.

The aces preferred to hunt alone, or in pairs.

If you were one of Britain's Allies or enemies in the First World War, to be a fighter ace meant that you had shot down five of the enemy in aerial combat. If you were British you had to shoot down ten!

Many fighter pilots on both sides had far higher scores than this. The 'ace of aces' was a German, Manfred von Richthofen, victor in eighty air battles before he himself was brought down with a bullet in his head. He was called 'the Red Baron'.

MANFRED VON RICHTHOFEN

One day, for no particular reason, I got the idea to paint my machine glaring red. After that, absolutely everyone knew my red bird. In fact, even my opponents were not completely unaware.

During a fight that occurred at another place on the Front, I succeeded in shooting down a two-seat Vickers that had been quite calmly photographing our artillery emplacements. My opponent never had a chance to turn and had to hasten to get down to earth, for he had already begun to show suspicious signs of burning. When a plane is in such a condition, we say: 'He stinks.' As it turned out, in fact, his time was up, for, shortly before the machine came to earth, it burst into bright flames.

I felt a deep compassion for my opponent and decided not to send him plunging down. I wanted to force him to land, for I had the feeling that he was already wounded. He did not fire a shot.

At about 500-metre altitude, a malfunction in my machine during a normal glide forced me also to land before making another turn. Now something quite comical happened. My enemy in his burning machine landed smoothly, while I, the victor, turned right over near him on the barbed wire of the trenches of a reserve emplacement.

A sporting reception followed with both Englishmen, who were more than a little surprised at my crash – for, as I mentioned, they had not fired a shot at me and they could not imagine why I had made a forced landing. These were the first Englishmen I had brought down alive. Therefore, I enjoyed talking with them. Among other things, I asked them if they had ever seen my machine in the air. 'Oh yes,' one of them said, 'I know it quite well. We call it *le petit rouge*.'

Then came what was, in my view, a typically English dirty trick. He asked my why I had acted so carelessly in landing. I told him the reason was that I could not do anything else. Then the scoundrel said that in the last 300 metres he had attempted to shoot at me, but his guns had jammed. I had given him a gift of his life. He took it and subsequently repaid me with an insidious personal attack.

Von Richthofen had assumed that the British were helpless and had surrendered; he was therefore correct in not
firing at them. The British did not know that he thought
this, and they assumed that he was coming in for the
kill.

Because of this unfortunate misunderstanding von
Richthofen became bitter and from then on always
finished off his opponent. *Le petit rouge* became *le diable
rouge*. When the Allied fighters began to concentrate
their attacks on his conspicuous red Albatross his whole
squadron painted their aeroplanes red. 'Richthofen's
Flying Circus' was composed of aces. If an Allied pilot
sighted red planes in his bit of sky he knew that he was in
for a real fight.

Frequently ace met ace. A famous Canadian fighter
pilot tells of a 'red-letter day' when he met the Red
Baron.

WILLIAM BISHOP

April 30th was a red-letter day for me. I celebrated it by
having a record number of fights in a given space of time.
In one hour and forty-five minutes I had nine separate
scraps. This was during the morning. Before we had tea
that afternoon, the major and I had a set-to with four
scarlet German scouts that was the most hair-raising encounter I have ever been mixed up in.

The many experiences of the morning had put me in a
good humour for fighting, and immediately the midday
meal was finished, I was up in the air again, with my
squadron commander, to see if there were any Huns
about looking for a bit of trouble. We patrolled along the
lines for twenty minutes, but saw nothing in that time.

Then, as I was leading, I headed farther into enemy territory, and presently, to the south of us, we saw five Albatross scouts. We went after them, but before we had come within firing distance, we discovered four red Albatrosses just to our right. This latter quartet, I believe, was made up of Baron von Richthofen and three of his best men.

However, although we knew who they were, we had been searching for a fight, and were feeling rather bored with doing nothing, so after the four we went. The major reached them first and opened fire on the rear machine from behind. Immediately the leader of the scouts did a lightning turn and came back at the major, firing at him and passing within two or three feet of his machine. In my turn I opened fire on the Baron, and in another half-moment found myself in the midst of what seemed to be a stampede of bloodthirsty animals. Everywhere I turned smoking bullets were jumping at me, and although I got in two or three good bursts at the Baron's 'red devil', I was rather bewildered for two or three minutes, as I could not see what was happening to the major and was not at all certain as to what was going to happen to me.

It was a decided difference from the fighting of the morning. The Germans seemed to be out to avenge their losses, and certainly were in fighting trim. Around we went in cyclonic circles for several minutes, here a flash of the Hun machines, then a flash of silver as my squadron commander would whizz by. All the time I would be in the same mix-up myself, every now and then finding a red machine in front of me and getting in a round or two of quick shots. I was glad the Germans were scarlet and we were silver. There was no need to hesitate about firing when the right colour flitted by your nose. It was a light-

*Everywhere I turned smoking bullets were
jumping at me*

ning fight, and I have never been in anything just like it.
Firing one moment, you would have to concentrate all
your mind and muscle the next in doing a quick turn to
avoid a collision. Once my gun jammed, and while
manoeuvring to the utmost of my ability to escape the
direct fire of one of the ravenous Germans, I had to 'fuss'
with the weapon until I got it right again. I had just got
going again when von Richthofen flashed by me and I let
him have a short burst. As I did so, I saw up above me
four more machines coming down to join in the fight.
Being far inside the German lines, I at once decided they
were additional Huns, so I 'zoomed' up out of the fight to
be free for a moment and have a look around. The
moment I did this I saw the approaching machines were
triplanes, belonging to one of our Naval squadrons, and
they were coming for all they were worth to help us
against the Albatrosses. The latter, however, had had
enough of the fight by now, and at the moment I
'zoomed' they dived and fled away towards the earth. I
did not know this until I looked down to where the fight
should still have been in progress. There was nothing to
be seen. Everybody had disappeared, including the major.
It was a sad moment for me, for I felt I had surely lost
him this time. After circling over the spot for five minutes
or more and exchanging signals with the triplanes, I
started for home with a heavy heart.

On the way I saw another machine approaching me,
and got into fighting position in the event it should prove
hostile. As we drew nearer together I recognized it as
another Nieuport, and then, to my great joy, I realized it
was the major. He had flown west at top speed as soon as
he saw the fight was over and I was not to be seen. He
was afraid I had followed the Huns down to the ground
in my excitement, and was very anxious as to what had

happened to me. Upon recognizing each other we waved
our hands in the air, then came close enough together to
exchange broad grins. We flew side by side to the aerodrome and landed. I found my machine had been very
badly shot about, one group of seven bullets having
passed within an inch of me in one place. It had been a
close shave, but a wonderful soul-stirring fight.

'Billy' Bishop survived the war to become the leading
living British ace, with a V C, DSO, MC, and a score of
seventy-two. The top British scorer, 'Mick' Mannock, had
been killed soon after his seventy-third victory.

The French ace Georges Guynemer, with a score of
fifty-four, failed to return from a patrol – shot down, it
was believed, by the observer of a German reconnaissance plane. The pilots of Guynemer's squadron went
out of their way, after this, to attack every enemy reconnaissance plane they sighted.

RENÉ FONCK

I was patrolling on September 30th, 1917, at an altitude
of 4,000 metres with several comrades, when I saw this
bold fellow flying below us. He calmly continued his inspection as though his life were somehow magically protected from danger. I immediately opened the throttle
and my Spad leaped forward. That Boche character did
not seem concerned at this, but upon approaching, I saw
his machine gun ready for action. The manoeuvre required close precision, but I was already an old hand at
this game. While still bearing down on him, I caused my
plane to make irregular movements similar to those

which permit a butterfly to escape its enemies, and my tactics evidently seemed to disconcert him.

I do not subscribe to the historic chivalrous attitude nor the lengths employed by Fontency in his offer to the enemy. This French commander was supposed to have said: 'Englishmen, you may fire first.' This, to my way of thinking, is a very impractical method. If the English had then had machine guns at their disposal, probably not a single Frenchman would have returned to report those gallant words. I believe it is necessary to adopt a middle-of-the-road attitude, not to waste my bullets but to fire away at the very moment when I have the best chance to score.

Therefore, without answering back, I accepted the fire of the Boche three times, but when my turn came and I fired my machine guns, I immediately had the satisfaction of seeing the enemy plane shudder. I went through some feints, and quickly coming out, I succeeded in placing myself under the rudder of my adversary. Almost simultaneously I caught both the pilot and machine gunner in my fire.

From above, I watched their fall. A thousand metres below me, perhaps, one of the plane's wings broke off, and the men were catapulted from their seats. I always felt a little compassion for my victims, despite the slightly animalistic satisfaction of having saved my own skin and the patriotic joy of victory.

I often preferred to spare their lives, especially when they fought bravely – but, as I believe I once said, in aerial combat there is usually no other alternative than victory or death, and it is rarely possible to give quarter to the enemy without betraying the interests of your country.

Thus, these latest Boches brought down had been admirable. Pilot and machine-gunner had not for a moment lost their composure, and seeing me approach, instead of disrupting their reconnaissance mission and turning tail for home at full speed, they had waited for me, courageously accepting combat without batting an eyelash.

No sooner did I land than I took a vehicle to go and see my victims and examine on the spot the remains of the plane to learn if the situation called for improvement in my technique. Some officers had preceded me, and the first news that they gave me was that one of the bodies carried papers identifying it as Wissemann, the very same one to whom the German newspapers gave credit as the victor over Guynemer.

By the end of the war René Fonck was the top French ace with seventy-five kills and another twenty unconfirmed.

There were American aces, serving with the Allied air squadrons, before the USA entered the war in 1917. One such was Raoul Lufbery. Early in 1918 he was given command of the first American fighter squadron in France, the 94th Aero Pursuit Squadron. His new pilots were very conscious that they had a long way to go if they were to match the performance of the aces who had, some of them, been fighting since 1914. One man who tried with all his might was:

EDWARD RICKENBACKER

In addition to leading my flight on routine patrols, I emulated Lufbery's example and flew my own lone-wolf missions over the lines. He always said that it was impossible to shoot down German planes sitting in the billet with your feet before the fire. I heeded his advice so well that I had more hours in the air than any other American flyer.

Reed Chambers was a close second. At night and on rainy days Reed and I would discuss combat flying by the hour. In this completely new arena of warfare, we were convinced that if we thought long enough and hard enough we could devise some new strategy, some new technique, that would mean the difference between victory and defeat, life and death. One night we had an idea that was so simple that we both wondered why no one had thought of it before. Our plan was simply to take off well before dawn, climb as high as our Nieuports would take us and hover high over the lines waiting for the first German plane to come by.

My orderly pulled me out of bed at four AM on a chilly May morning. Reed and I met in the Mess hall for some scalding coffee, then went out into the lines where our shivering mechanics were warming up our planes, climbed into our fur-lined suits and took off. We pushed our little ships up to 18,000 feet. At that altitude, with our bare faces sticking out of the cockpits, the temperature was below zero.

Despite the numbing cold and the slight dizziness brought on by the altitude and our empty stomachs, we waited and waited, two specks in the sky three and a half miles over no-man's-land, patiently patrolling our sector. Dawn came on a beautiful cloudless day. Our scheme had worked perfectly: the only thing wrong was that the unpredictable Boches did not take advantage of these perfect conditions to photograph our lines.

I had about an hour's fuel left. At the aerodrome the other fellows were sitting down to a table loaded with hot food. Lufbery had said that you could not shoot down Germans at the breakfast table; well, those fellows were shooting down as many as I was, and they were warm besides.

Apparently Reed had given up and gone home. I was one lone speck in the sky. Why not try a better hunting ground? Twenty-five miles to the east was the famous old fortress city of Metz, with a German aerodrome nearby. I climbed to 20,000 feet, seeing the first red arc of the rising sun, and headed into German territory. I felt invulnerable. Though the Germans manning the anti-aircraft batteries below me could probably hear the sound of my engine, I was sure that they could not see me five miles up in the bright morning sky.

I flew over Metz several times, paying special attention to the aerodrome, but the Germans simply were not flying that day. Not much gas remained, but I decided to make one last check at a field near Thiaucourt. Still at 20,000 feet, I cut off my engine to save fuel. As I silently circled the field, like a great bird of prey, I saw, far beneath me, three graceful German Albatrosses taxi out on to the field and take off, one by one. They headed straight southwards, climbing steadily, obviously unaware of my presence above them.

I continued circling, afraid even to breathe, until the last of the three was well on its way, with his back towards me. I put the little Nieuport into a shallow dive to start the propeller going and turned on the ignition. The engine caught, and I gunned my plane after the three Germans. I hoped to time it so that I would make my attack over the lines, rather than over German territory.

Closer, closer. My eyes were glued on the leather-jacketed shoulders of the German flying the rearmost Albatross. That is where my bullets were going to go. I was so intent on the pursuit that I completely forgot about a German stratagem. In front of the planes ahead, but higher, a black puff appeared in the sky, then another and another. The German batteries had seen me, and it was their way of warning the three planes in front of me. They were setting the fuse so that the shell would burst at approximately my altitude.

The pilot in front of me turned his head to look behind him. I saw the sun glint off his glasses. All pilots immediately put their planes into a dive. I was now within 200 yards of the last plane, and I had no intention of letting him get away. I knew the Nieuport's fatal weakness of shedding its wing covering in a dive, but in the excitement I did not think of it at all. I gunned the plane up to a speed of at least 150mph and closed in on the man in front of me.

At fifty yards I gave him a ten-second burst of machine gun fire. I saw the bullets hit the back of his seat. I felt no sympathy. He had made a stupid mistake in diving rather than trying to outmanoeuvre me.

By then the other two pilots had had an excellent opportunity to pull up and get on my tail. At that moment either of them could be sighting down my back. But I still wanted to make sure that I had killed my man. Not until I saw his plane go out of control did I try to pull my own out of the dive. I had to come out of it in a hurry, put the ship into a sharp climb and have it out with the other two. I pulled the stick back into my lap.

A ripping, tearing crash shook the plane. The entire spread of linen over the right upper wing was stripped off by the force of the wind. I manipulated the controls, but it did no good. The plane turned over on her right side. The tail was forced up. The left wing came around. The ship was in a tailspin. With the nose down, the tail began revolving to the right, faster and faster. It was death. I had not lost my willingness to fight to live, but in that situation there was not much I could do. Even birds need two wings to fly.

The two remaining Albatrosses began diving at me, one after the other, pumping bullets into my helpless Nieuport. I was not angry at the two men for trying to kill me; I simply thought that they were stupid. Why waste ammunition? Did they think I was playing possum, with the framework of one wing hanging in the breeze?

A crippled plane can take a long time to flutter to earth. I wondered exactly how I would die. Would the plane shake itself to pieces? In that case, I would go whistling down to hit the ground and splatter. If the plane stayed in one piece, it might crash in the trees beneath me, and I might only break a few bones. Which announcement would my mother prefer to read in the telegram from the War Department – that I was dead or that I was injured behind the lines?

I began remembering all the major episodes of my life, the good things I had done and the bad things. The bad seemed to outnumber the good. And then I remembered the Lord above.

'Oh, God,' I prayed, 'help me get out of this.'

The earth was coming up fast. Without thinking, almost as though I were moved by something bigger than myself, I pulled open the throttle. The sudden extra speed lifted the nose of the plane. For a second there, I was horizontal. I pulled on the joystick and reversed the rudder. I must have hit the one combination in a million that would work. The fuselage remained almost horizontal. The nose was heading for the American lines only a couple of miles away. If I could only hold her like that, I might make it.

I was at less than 2,000 feet, and every anti-aircraft battery, every machine gunner and practically every rifleman began sending a curtain of lead into the sky. I flew right on through it. I had no choice.

I talked to that little plane all the way home. Losing altitude, with the engine going full blast and the controls jammed in the only position that enabled it to stay aloft, my little plane and I crossed the lines. When I reached the field, I was flying at treetop height. I could not cut back the engine, for then I'd go straight down. I came in for my landing with the engine running wide open. Everybody dashed out to see what fool was coming in at full throttle. I grazed the top of the hangar, pancaked down on the ground and slid to a stop in a cloud of dust. I swung out of the bullet-riddled, battered little crate and tried to saunter nonchalantly towards the hangar as though I came in like that every day.

Reed came in for a landing a minute later. We walked in together. I felt calm. But, when I was alone in front of my bunk, suddenly my knees turned to water. The next thing I knew I was sitting down.

Before the year was out the war was over. Rickenbacker had overtaken Lufbery and was the leading American ace with twenty-six confirmed victories to his credit. He had succeeded Lufbery in command of the 94th Squadron which was by then called the 'Hat-in-the-ring' Squadron because their planes was adorned with an insignia of Uncle Sam's stovepipe hat, starred and striped, inside a ring. (Throwing one's hat into the ring is a challenge to fight.)

For ease of recognition by trigger-happy ground troops, Allied planes were distinguished by roundels painted on the wings and fuselage. The French roundel – counting from the outer circle – was red, white and blue; the British was blue, white and red; and the American blue, red and white.

The Germans used a black Maltese cross, both as the insignia on their aeroplanes and as the design of the Iron Cross decoration. In the Second World War they used a straight-sided black cross and the Nazi swastika. Now, in NATO, they have reverted to the Maltese cross.

Between the wars the USA changed their emblem to a white star on a blue circle ground.

CHAPTER FOUR

Blitzkrieg in Europe

Germany lost the First World War, and the Versailles Peace Treaty forbade her a military air force. To get round the ban the Germans designed and built a large fleet of commercial aircraft and sports planes which could be converted quickly for military use. Gliding clubs were formed where young men were taught to fly. By secret agreement with the USSR, aircrews and their planes were smuggled into Russia to continue training at a special aerodrome not far from Moscow. Thus, even before Hitler came into power in 1933, Germany had the beginnings of a big new military air force.

Still in secret, Hitler inaugurated the *Luftwaffe*. Pilots disguised as civilians were now sent to train in Italy where Mussolini had the most up-to-date Air Force in Europe. By 1935 Hitler felt strong enough to announce publicly the formation of the *Luftwaffe* and the appointment of Hermann Goering, fighter ace of the First World War, as *Generaldeflieger*.

The 'new' *Luftwaffe* already had modern aircraft and well-trained men to fly them. All it needed was combat experience. When the Spanish Civil War broke out in 1936 Goering was quick to seize the opportunity. He formed the *Kondor* Legion under the command of Wolfram von Richthofen, cousin of the Red Baron, and dispatched it to Spain to support the insurgent Fascists. Here the Me 109 fighter, the Ju 87 'Stuka' dive-bomber, the He 111 medium bomber and the Dornier 107 'flying pencil' heavy bomber were all tried out in war conditions. New inventions were tested, for example the radio telephone. The patrol leader could now speak to the pilots in his flight instead of conveying orders by waggling wings, diving, zooming, or firing coloured flares; and he in turn could be directed by radio messages from the ground.

In Spain, German war strategy and tactics were developed. As a deliberate experiment an open (undefended) town, Guernica, was devastated from the air. Formations of German fighters machine gunned the people in the streets and market-place; then wave after wave of bombers flew low over the houses releasing their loads of high-explosive and incendiary bombs. More than 1,600 civilians were killed, and the survivors made homeless.

Few people in England recognized the threat posed by Hitler's military dictatorship. The Royal Air Force (formed in 1918 from the RFC and the RNAS) had no experience of modern aerial warfare. Its aircraft were obsolete, slower and less heavily armed than the *Luftwaffe*'s.

R. J. Mitchell, the designer of the Supermarine S6B with which in 1931 Britain had won outright the Schneider Trophy and created a world air-speed record of 406.99 mph, was one of the few who realized the danger. On a skiing holiday in Kitzbuhel, Austria, in 1934, he had met officers of the ambitious expanding *Luftwaffe*. He returned home convinced that Germany was already planning another war against England. Using his S6B as a starting point, he went to work and designed the famous Spitfire fighter which, with the Hawker Hurricane, was to save Britain from the same fate as Czechoslovakia,

Poland, Denmark, Norway, Holland, Belgium, Luxembourg, and France.

When Hitler occupied Czechoslovakia in 1938, Britain was not ready to fight and played for time. A year later he launched his first *Blitzkrieg* (lightning war) against Poland. We were still not ready but we declared war, and so did France.

The French, expecting ground battles like those of the First World War, had built the formidable Maginot Line – fortifications stretching from the Belgian border to Switzerland. The British Army supplied a large Expeditionary Force to man the French frontier north of the Maginot Line to the sea. The R A F sent a few squadrons of Hurricane fighters and Blenheim bombers, as many as could be spared in view of an expected German attack on the British Isles.

There was very little fighting in the first winter of the war. The R A F hunted submarines, dropped a few small bombs on German ports and shipping, sowed mines in the North Sea, and scattered pamphlets urging the Germans to surrender (in the belief that the populace as a whole was not Nazi). The soldiers of the British Expeditionary Force dug themselves in and got rather bored.

An American senator dismissed the war as 'phoney'. The French called it '*la drôle de guerre*'.

Then spring came, and Hitler launched his biggest *Blitzkrieg* yet. He invaded Denmark, Norway, and the Low Countries. These small neutral nations could not hold out for long against the *Luftwaffe* dive-bombers and the fast moving tanks of the *Panzer* divisions. By early May the might of Germany was concentrated against France. The Maginot Line was outflanked. The military retreat, which was to end for Britain on the beaches of Dunkirk, began.

Hopelessly outnumbered, the Allied Air Forces did their best.

The RAF had ten Hurricane fighter squadrons based in Eastern France – so few, compared to the *Luftwaffe*, that when the *Blitzkrieg* began, Air Headquarters decreed that the fighters' primary job was to escort friendly bombers, not to attack enemy raiders. Policy changed when the city of Rheims (where AHQ was based) was bombed. Nº I Fighter Squadron led by Johnny Walker was ordered into the air to engage a second big formation of Dorniers heading for the city. A Hurricane pilot describes the battle:

PAUL RICHEY

Approaching Sedan Johnny called: 'There they are! There they are! Straight ahead!' I couldn't see them at first, but suddenly I did, and my heart raced. As we came nearer I counted them – thirty Dorniers in two squadrons of fifteen more or less in line abreast, covered by fifteen 110s in groups of twos and threes wheeling and zig-zagging slowly above, ahead, beside and behind the bombers. They were going west across our noses from right to left.

Johnny rocked his wings for us to close in tighter and pressed straight on, climbing a little to 7,000 feet, then turning left and diving at the Huns from astern. 'Now keep in – keep in – and keep a bloody good lookout!' he said steadily. I was swivel-eyed as we approached, to make sure we were not being attacked by something unseen, for the Huns continued straight on although we were closing on them. They must have seen us long before, but it was not until the last moment that the 110s wheeled, some to the right and some to the left, going into aircraft-line-astern in twos and threes.

We went in fast in a tight bunch, each picking a 110 and manoeuvring to get on his tail. I selected the rear one of two in line-astern who were turning tightly to the left. He broke away from his No 1 when he had done a half-circle and steepened his turn, but I easily turned inside him, holding my fire until I was within fifty yards and then firing a shortish burst at three-quarter deflection. To my surprise a mass of bits flew off him – pieces of engine cowling and lumps of his glass-house (hood) – and as I passed just over the top of him, still in a left-hand turn, I watched with a kind of fascinated horror as he went into a spin, smoke pouring out of him. I remember saying 'My God, how ghastly!' as his tail suddenly swivelled sideways and tore off, while flames streamed over the fuselage. Then, I saw a little white parachute open beside it. Good!

Scarcely half a minute had passed, yet as I looked quickly around me I saw four more 110s go down – one with its tail off, a second in a spin, a third vertically in flames, and a fourth going up at forty-five degrees in a left-hand stall turn with a little Hurricane on its tail firing into its side, from which burst a series of flashes and long shooting red flames. I shall never forget it.

All the 110s at my level were hotly engaged, so I searched above. 'Yes – those beggars up there will be a nuisance soon!' Three cunning chaps were out of the fight, climbing like mad in line-astern to get above us to pounce. I had plenty of ammunition left, so I climbed after them with the boost-override pulled. They were in a slight right-hand turn, and as I climbed I looked around. There were three others over on the right coming towards me, but they were below. I reached the rear 110 of the three above me. He caught fire after a couple of bursts and went down in flames. Then I dived at the tri-

nity coming up from the fight and fired a quick burst at
the leader head-on.

I turned, but they were still there: so were the other
two from above. In a moment I was in the centre of what
seemed a stack of 110s, although there were in fact only

*He caught fire after a couple of bursts and went
down in flames*

five. I knew I hadn't the speed or height in my wooden-
blader to dive away and beat it, so I decided to stay and
make the best of it. Although I was more manoeuvrable
at this height than the Huns, I found it impossible to get
an astern shot in because every time I almost got one lined
up, tracers came whipping past from another on my tail.
All I could do was keep twisting and turning, and when a

110 got behind me make as tight a turn as possible, almost spinning, with full engine, and fly straight at him, firing a quick burst, then push the stick forward and dive under his nose. I would then pull up in a steep climbing turn to meet the next gentleman.

Obviously they couldn't all attack at once without colliding, but several times I was at the apex of a cone formed by the cannon and machine-gun fire of three of them. Their tactics consisted mostly of diving, climbing and taking full deflection shots at me. Their shooting seemed wild. This manoeuvre was easily dealt with by turning towards them and popping over their heads, forcing them to steepen their climb until they stalled and had to fall away. But I was not enjoying this marathon. Far from it. My mouth was getting drier and drier, and I was feeling more and more desperate and exhausted. Would they run out of ammunition? Would they push off? Would help come? I knew I couldn't hold out much longer.

After what seemed an age (actually it turned out to be fifteen minutes, which is an exceptionally long time for a dogfight) I was flying down head-on at a 110 who was climbing up to me. We both fired – and I thought I had left it too late and we would collide. I pushed the stick forwards violently. There was a stunning explosion right in front of me. For an instant my mind went blank. My aircraft seemed to be falling, limp on the controls. Then as black smoke poured out of the nose and enveloped the hood, and a hot blast and a flicker of reflected flame crept into the dark cockpit, I said 'Come on – out you go!' pulled the pin out of my harness, wrenched open the hood and hauled myself head-first out to the right.

The wind pressed me tightly against the side of the aircraft, my legs still inside. I caught hold of the trailing edge of the wing and heaved myself out. As I fell free and somersaulted I felt as if a giant had me on the end of a length of wire, whirling me round and round through the air. I fumbled for and pulled the rip-cord and was pulled right way up with a violent jerk that winded me. My head was pressed forwards by the parachute back-pad that had slipped up behind me, and I couldn't look up to see if the parachute was OK. I had no sensation of movement – just a slight breeze as I swung gently to and fro. For all I knew the thing might be on fire or not properly open.

I heard the whirr of Hun engines and saw three of the 110s circle me. I looked at the ground and saw a shower of flaming sparks as something exploded in an orchard far below: my late aeroplane.

The Hun engines faded and died. I rolled the rip-cord round its D-ring and put it in my pocket as a souvenir. I was still bloody frightened, as I was smack over a wood and thought I'd probably break my legs if I landed in it; and I confess without shame that I reeled off several prayers, both of thanks and supplication, as I dangled in the air. I was soon low enough to see my drift. It was towards a village, and it looked as though I might clear the trees only to hit a roof. But no – it was to be the wood all right. I was very low now, swinging gently. I saw two French motor-cycle troops running along the road, first one way, then the other. I waved to them. The trees rushed up at me. Now for it! I relaxed completely, shutting my eyes calmly. There was a swish of branches and a bump as I did a back-somersault on the ground. I had fallen between the trees.

I jumped up as the two French soldiers came crashing through the trees, one with a revolver in his hand and the other carrying a rifle. '*Haut les mains!*' they shouted, pointing their weapons at me. I raised my arms as they advanced cautiously. I was wearing white overalls over my uniform, and still had my helmet and oxygen mask on. I spoke through the mask with difficulty. They refused to believe I was English, but I eventually managed to persuade them to look for the RAF wings under my overalls. Having done this, they put down their weapons and embraced me warmly.

I tore off my helmet and threw it on the ground, shouting 'Ces salauds de Boches!' which relieved my feelings slightly. We gathered up my parachute and moved on to the village. I rode in the side-car of their motor-cycle combination. The entire population of Rumigny had witnessed the fight and had seen six Huns come down nearby; they had watched me fighting the remaining five and said it had lasted at least fifteen minutes, perhaps more.

When I got back to the Squadron I found that Johnny claimed to have shot down one definitely, and perhaps two, Hilly two, Killy two and Soper two. With my two that made exactly the number found – ten – leaving the number I had fought as five (total fifteen as counted before the fight). The villagers on the ground had seen two enemy tails come off – presumably one was mine; the other was Killy's. The police presented me with one of the fins – with the black-and-white swastika pierced by two bullets, it made a respectable match for the two First War fins we had with the Black Cross emblems on them.

The French were enthusiastic over our victory, and I was encouraged to hear that the thirty Dorniers had turned and beetled off when we tackled their fighter escort.

N° 1 Fighter Squadron lived up to its name. It was the first to score 100 victories, during the Battle of France. In only ten days in May Richey and his fellow pilots destroyed 114 enemy aircraft in combat. Their own losses during those ten days were two pilots killed, two wounded, and one taken prisoner of war.

The Squadron was awarded ten DFCs and three DFMs for gallantry in this Battle. One of the DFCs went to Paul Richey. In a later action than the one he describes here he shot down three Heinkel bombers before he himself was put out of action. He crash-landed, badly wounded, and it was eleven months before he was fit to fight again.

The RAF lost a quarter of its total fighter force in the defence of France and in providing cover for the retreating Expeditionary Force. Most were destroyed on the ground and not in combat.

CHAPTER FIVE

The Battle of Britain

The Battle of Britain was the greatest air battle that has ever been fought.

Hitler had intended to continue his *Blitzkrieg* on into the British Isles just as soon as he had established military bases and aerodromes along the coasts of Holland, Belgium, and Northern France; but during the Battle of France the *Luftwaffe* had been challenged for the first time. He and Goering decided that before crossing the Channel they must wipe out the RAF.

They reckoned that it would take the *Luftwaffe* one week to destroy the RAF squadrons based in the south of England, and four more weeks to deal with the remainder of Britain's air defences. Then Operation *Seelowe* (Sea Lion), the invasion and conquest of Britain, could begin. The code name they gave to the day the *Luftwaffe* launched its massive strike against the RAF was *Adlertag* – Eagle Day.

The Nazi leaders had left three vital factors out of their reckoning: the spirit of the RAF, the stoicism of the British people, and the inventive genius of her 'Boffins' (as her designers and scientists were nicknamed). The Hurricane was a good fighter aircraft, the Spitfire was better, and the RAF had radar to help them.

Like several other scientific discoveries, such as penicillin, radar had been discovered almost by accident. In the early thirties the Post Office had found that passing aeroplanes interfered with and reflected their radio signals. An Air Ministry committee asked the Scottish scientist R. A. Watson-Watt whether this physical fact could be used to produce a lethal ray which would destroy hostile aircraft. He said no; what it would do was detect them and give their bearing and range. By the outbreak of war British RDF – Radio Direction Finding as it was called until 1943 – was already far in advance of a similar German invention.

The months of the Phoney War and the few brief weeks between the fall of France and *Adlertag* gave the Government enough time to complete a chain of radar stations at intervals along the south-eastern coasts of England.

When the 'blips' caused by hostile aircraft entering the area appeared on the cathode tubes of the radar screens, the operators passed on the vital details to Control HQ, the duty controller called up the fighter stations nearest to the enemy, and the pilots took to the air.

Acting on information from the radar stations, WAAF plotters at HQ illustrated the course of the battle by moving counters – red for the enemy, black for our own machines – on the operations room map table. The controller, watching the course of the battle on the map, was able to direct the fighters in the air by radio telephone.

A simple code was used: HAYWIRE TO RED LEADER SCRAMBLE FIFTY PLUS BANDITS ANGELS FIFTEEN VECTOR ONE SEVEN ZERO BUSTER was understood to mean CONTROLLER CALLING LEADER OF RED SECTION – TAKE TO THE AIR IMMEDIATELY – THERE ARE MORE THAN FIFTY ENEMY AIRCRAFT APPROACHING AT A HEIGHT OF FIFTEEN THOUSAND

FEET — YOU SHOULD STEER COURSE OF 170 DEGREES AT FULL SPEED TO INTERCEPT THEM.

When the fighters sighted the enemy they called TALLY HO! over the radio telephone and if the controller wanted his pilots to return and land he would say PANCAKE!

The Boffins with their new inventions and aircraft designs, the factory workers who worked long shifts round the clock to produce them, the ground staffs at the aerodromes and radar sites — these and countless others helped to win the Battle of Britain.

The actual fighting was done by the gallant young men whom Churchill christened 'The Few'. Not all were British. Among them were some Americans who had refused to wait for the USA to enter the war, and many Allied airmen who had refused to surrender when their countries were overrun, and had managed to escape to England so that they could fight on.

Against this opposition the *Luftwaffe* did its damnedest; and it failed.

First the dive-bombing Stukas attacked Channel coastal shipping, not because this was a vital target but in order to tempt the RAF fighters into the sky where lurking swarms of Messerschmitts were, in theory, to exterminate them. When the losses of Stukas and Messerschmitts began to mount up, the next phase began. The *Luftwaffe* attacked the RAF on the ground and in the air over the Southern Marches of England.

The weather, that late summer of 1940, was perfect. Thanks to radar the fighter pilots did not have to waste time, energy, and fuel in useless patrols. Often they could wait in the sun on the dry grass near their aircraft until bandits appeared on the radar screens and Control gave the order to scramble.

The enemy raiders came in vast formations.

Hornchurch aerodrome had been bombed at midday. An experienced maintenance sergeant and his fitters had been killed. The landing strip had been cratered like the surface of the moon. The CO mustered all available personnel, RAF and WAAF, to fill in the holes. By the evening the aerodrome was fully 'serviceable' again. The pilots of 603 Spitfire Squadron, led by 'Uncle George' Denholm, were playing poker in the Mess when the voice of the controller came over the loudspeaker:

RICHARD HILLARY

'603 Squadron take off and patrol base: further instructions in the air.'

We made a dash for our machines and within two minutes were off the ground. Twice we circled the aerodrome to allow all twelve planes to get in formation. We were flying in four sections of three: Red Section leading, Blue and Green to right and left, and the three remaining planes forming a guard section above and behind us.

I was flying No 2 in the Blue section.

Over the radio came the voice of the controller: 'Hullo, Red leader,' followed by instructions on course and height.

As always, for the first few minutes we flew on the reciprocal of the course given until we reached 15,000 feet. We then turned about and flew on 110° in an all-out climb, thus coming out of the sun and gaining height all the way.

During the climb Uncle George was in constant touch with the ground. We were to intercept about twenty enemy fighters at 25,000 feet. I glanced across at Stapme

and saw his mouth moving. That meant he was singing again. He would sometimes do this with his radio set on 'send' with the result that, mingled with our instructions from the ground, we would hear a raucous rendering of *Night and Day*. And then quite clearly over the radio I heard the Germans excitedly calling to each other. This was a not infrequent occurrence and it made one feel that they were right behind, although often they were some distance away. I switched my set to 'send' and called out '*Halt's Maul!*' and as many other choice pieces of German invective as I could remember. To my delight I heard one of them answer: 'You feelthy Englishman, we will teach you how to speak to a German.'

I looked down. It was a completely cloudless sky and way below lay the English countryside, stretching lazily into the distance, a quite extraordinary picture of green and purple in the setting sun.

I took a glance at my altimeter. We were at 28,000 feet. At that moment Sheep yelled 'Tallyho' and dropped down in front of Uncle George in a slow dive in the direction of the approaching planes. Uncle George saw them at once.

'OK. Line astern.'

I drew in behind Stapme and took a look at them. They were about 2,000 feet below us, which was a pleasant change, but they must have spotted us at the same moment, for they were forming a protective circle, one behind the other, which is a defence formation hard to break.

'Echelon starboard,' came Uncle George's voice.

We spread out fanwise to the right.

'Going down!'

One after the other we peeled off in a power dive. I picked out one machine and switched my gun-button to

'Fire'. At 300 yards I had him in my sights. At 200 I opened up in a long four-second burst and saw the tracer going into his nose. Then I was pulling out, so hard that I could feel my eyes dropping through my neck. Coming round in a slow climbing turn, I saw that we had broken them up. The sky was now a mass of individual dogfights. Several of them had already been knocked down. One I hoped was mine, but on pulling up I had not been able to see the result. To my left I saw Peter Pease make a head-on attack on a Messerschmitt. They were headed straight for each other and it looked as though the fire of both was striking home. Then at the last moment the Messer-schmitt pulled up, taking Peter's fire full in the belly. It rolled on to its back, yellow flames pouring from the cockpit, and vanished.

The next few minutes were typical. First the sky a bedlam of machines; then suddenly silence and not a plane to be seen. I noticed then that I was very tired and very hot. The sweat was running down my face in rivu-lets. But this was no time for vague reflections. Flying around the sky on one's own at that time was not a healthy course of action.

I still had some ammunition left. Having no desire to return to the aerodrome until it had all been used to some good purpose, I took a look around the sky for some friendly fighters. About a mile away over Dungeness I saw a formation of about forty Hurricanes on patrol at 20,000 feet. Feeling that there was safety in numbers, I set off in their direction. When about 200 yards from the rear machine, I looked down and saw 5,000 feet below another formation of fifty machines flying in the same direction. Flying stepped up like this was an old trick of the Huns, and I was glad to see we were adopting the same tactics. But as though hit by a douche of cold water,

I suddenly woke up. There far more machines flying together than we could ever muster over one spot. I took another look at the rear machine in my formation, and sure enough, there was the swastika on its tail. Yet they all seemed quite oblivious of my presence. I had the sun behind me and a glorious opportunity. Closing in to 150 yards I let go a three-second burst into the rear machine. It flicked on to its back and spun out of sight. Feeling like an irresponsible schoolboy who has perpetrated some crime which must inevitably be found out, I glanced round me. Still nobody seemed disturbed. I suppose I could have repeated the performance on the next machine, but I felt that it was inadvisable to tempt Providence too far. I did a quick half-roll and made off home, where I found to my irritation that Raspberry, as usual, had three planes down to my one.

Many Battle of Britain fighter pilots were killed, either in that battle or later in the war. Richard Hillary, within a few days of the dogfight he describes here, baled out badly burned into the North Sea and survived the ordeal and months in hospital only to be killed after his return to active service.

CHAPTER SIX

The Blitz

Sunday September 15th, 1940, was the day the RAF demonstrated that the *Luftwaffe* was not, after all, invincible. On that day the Germans flew over 1,300 sorties and lost fifty-six aircraft to the RAF's twenty-six.

Although there were still a lot of German aircraft left and a lot more to come from factories scattered throughout the *Reich*, Hitler was becoming impatient. His invasion barges, which were waiting in the ports and canals and rivers of North-western Europe, were being destroyed by RAF bombers before they could be used. He decided that he would get quicker results by bombing London and other major cities. If the *Luftwaffe* terrorized the civilians, they would flee in panic and cause chaos on the roads, the Royal Family and the Government would evacuate to Canada, the British Empire would collapse; and the invading *Panzer* divisions would have their usual picnic.

Goering sent wave after wave of heavy bombers to attack the cities, and in spite of the RAF and the ground defences many got through. In September and October, in the 'Blitz' on London alone, 13,000 were killed and more than 20,000 injured. The thought of surrender never entered the citizens' minds. They were now in the front line and in a gruesome way they enjoyed it.

During the daylight raids RAF fighters and anti-aircraft gunners continued to take a heavy toll of the German bombers and their escorting Messerschmitts, but at night, except at full moon with a clear sky, the fighters found it difficult to make contact with the enemy. Ground Control could guide them into the general vicinity of the bandits; from then on good visibility was essential. Pilots with extraordinarily good night vision could and did score some successes, but the vast majority of the raiders were able to drop their bombs unmolested except by AA fire.

The Boffins came up with a new radar device – AI or Aircraft Interception. This short-range set, fitted into the night fighter itself, enabled an aircrew operator to take over from Ground Control and direct his pilot the last few thousand feet on to the target.

To help Control distinguish between friend and foe the night fighters were also fitted with IFF (Identification Friend or Foe), a small transmitting set which sent out a continuous signal.

War in the air was becoming complicated. The new airman had to do more than simply fly and fight. He had to be a highly skilled technician who could operate and even repair sophisticated instruments. The old days of Cecil Lewis and his primitive plate camera had gone for ever.

Under night-raid conditions each ground controller handled no more than two fighters at a time. The night boys had a language of their own: Bandits were 'customers' and the 'shop' was the particular sector of the sky for which the controller and his fighters were responsible.

The new invention had its teething troubles, as explained here by the radar operator of a Beaufighter piloted by John Cunningham.

C. F. 'JIMMY' RAWNSLEY

March, so far as I was concerned, was a terrible month. There were plenty of customers, and all I had was a long torment of fading blips and finger trouble. Several times moonlight and wandering searchlights betrayed us to the enemy, and then I was much too slow off the mark to be able to follow the panic dives of the alerted bombers. Throughout one unhappy sortie patrolling Spithead we spent the entire time trying to get a firm hold on a series of ghost echoes which could have been caused by any one of a multitude of indefinable things. And all the time a rain of bombs smashed and burned out the heart of Plymouth. Some days later Gilfillan (the Special Signals officer) managed to locate an obscure fault in the set.

But it could not go on for ever. Patient servicing and determined practice, I felt, must eventually pay off. And they did, one night early in April, when we had the satisfaction of seeing every cog in the complex machine working smoothly and efficiently.

We were among the last due to take off on the programme for that night, and a host of customers had already streamed in through the shop by the time we were called upon to serve them. Climbing up through a turbulent mass of cloud, we eventually broke through into the clear skies lit only by the light of the stars and a young moon. The pale glow made the ghostly cloudscape look like a lot of drifting icebergs. We headed for the coast, and John called up the GCI.

'Hullo, Starlight. This is Blazer Two Four calling. Are you receiving me?'

All formality vanished with the sound of Brownie's warm friendly voice replying: 'Good evening, John.' It was quite unhurried. 'I think we've got a customer for you. Angels ten and stand by.'

It was almost as if Brownie had just moved his stool two places along a well-lighted bar and was signalling to the landlord to take our order. I thought of what it was in reality, and I could see the draughty caravan and the flapping canvas, and plotters working with chilled fingers over their computers.

Brownie began to give us vectors in his usual sure and informative way, turning us to cut off the retreat of a homeward-bound bandit, what we used to call a 're-turned empty'.

'He'll be crossing starbound to port,' Brownie reported. 'Range two miles. Turn port on to . . .'

It appeared on the tubes of my own set, and I cut him short as I called to John over the intercom:

'Contact . . . 7,000 feet . . . turn to port.'

We were used to jinking targets by now. This one seemed to be following no set pattern, just wandering southwards in easy, haphazard curves. I cut the corners in order to close in faster, and had just slowed down for the final stalk when I had to leave the set to make an adjustment to the IFF. During the few seconds I was away John caught a glimpse of the engine exhausts of the bomber drifting across at fairly close range. But they quickly disappeared, and he throttled back and waited for me to take up the story again where I had left off.

The blip was still there, only 2,000 feet away. We closed in to half that range. And then John said:

'OK. You can have a look.'

I swivelled around and I saw our bird, already taking the familiar shape of a Heinkel as John cautiously moved in below it. But that was not what caught my attention. What took my breath away was the fantastic setting of the scene. All around us there towered great mountains of billowing cumulo-nimbus cloud, and the Heinkel was winding its way between their snowy, moonlit crests. We were sneaking along behind and below it in the darkened valley between what looked like mighty cliffs of ice. Now I understood the reason for those erratic curves. That German pilot was not going to endure the discomfort of flying through a turbulent cumulo-nimbus cloud when he could go round it.

A violent thunderstorm was raging in the depths of that heaving turmoil of cloud, and every few seconds the lightning flashed across, lighting the whole scene with a horrible, steel-blue clarity. We could see clear-cut every detail of the Heinkel. Surely, I thought, their gunners must be able to see us just as plainly as we could see them. We were barely a hundred yards away. As we crept in, each flash of lightning was a stab at the nerves, and as the darkness leaped back over us I sighed with relief. The Heinkel rode on, beautiful, serene, and unheeding. Finally we were right below it, ready to attack.

'OK?' John asked.

'Yes,' I replied. 'Hold your hat on.'

'Right. In we go!'

Slowly, very slowly, the Heinkel sank towards our sights. This was their gunner's chance just before we could bring our cannon to bear. We were a sitting duck, only eighty yards away, and in moonlight. Pale-blue exhaust flames licked along the engine cowling of the bomber, and John, in his calm, detached way, noticed that the outboard flames were on a lower level than those inboard.

Our aircraft wriggled nervously as John brought the gunsight on to his target. Then he opened fire, and almost at once the whole sky ahead of us seemed to dissolve in

flame. My knees caved in as the floor heaved underfoot.
Every slot and chink in the hull was lit by the lurid glow
of the sea of fire from the exploding Heinkel as we
ploughed on through it. Things bumped and scraped

Things bumped and scraped along outside . . .

along outside. And then we were through it all and out
into the darkness. My eardrums and breathing relaxed,
and I became conscious again of the reassuring roar of
our own engines. We still seemed to be flying.

'Are we all in one piece?' I asked.

'Yes . . . I think so,' John replied. His voice was still
quite calm as he took stock, methodically checking over

his instruments. 'Let's see now. Oil pressures . . . tempera-
tures . . . yes . . . everything seems to be all right.'

There had come back into our Beaufighter the typical
smell of a burning German aircraft, a smell that was to
make a deep and most unpleasant impression on me. It
was sweet and sickly, and came, I understood, from the
light alloy in the airframe as it burned. Others had re-
marked on that smell and we all found it rather naus-
eating.

I looked out quickly over our starboard quarter, and
there I saw a terrible sight. The shattered Heinkel, with
only one wing left, was spinning down vertically, spew-
ing out as it went a helix of burning petrol. It looked like
a gigantic catherine wheel, and I watched until it plunged
into the floor of the cloud below. The snows flurried and
glowed from within for a few seconds, and then it was all
swallowed up by the cloud. The severed wing fluttered
slowly down, a falling leaf spilling out drops of flame.
Then that, too, disappeared into the cloud, and we sailed
on alone. Two miles below us the icy black water of the
Channel would be quenching that dreadful fire.

A few nights later the same team shot down three customers in one night. Their score mounted steadily. Since
the radar set was on the secret list the Air Ministry hinted
that the successful pilot ate carrots to improve his night
vision. The newspapers christened him 'Cat's-Eyes' Cunningham.

CHAPTER SEVEN

The High Seas Fleet

The *Lutwaffe*'s all-out attempt to control the skies over Britain ended in April 1941 when Hitler abandoned Operation Sea Lion and turned his attention to the Balkans. He had already bullied Hungary, Rumania, and Bulgaria into reluctant military alliance with Nazi Germany. Yugoslavia refused to fall into line. Another *Blitzkrieg* was necessary. On Palm Sunday the *Luftwaffe* bombed the Yugoslav capital, Belgrade, killing 17,000 of its citizens. Within weeks the *Panzer* divisions had rumbled south through Serbia and Macedonia, and taken Greece.

Confident again after these easy victories, Hitler attacked the Soviet Union. At first the battle went his way, but the Russians soon rallied. Helped by shipments of vital war supplies from Britain, and by the appalling cold of the Russian winter, they fought back.

Now Britain had the USSR to help in the fight against the Axis powers. In December that year that third member of the Axis, Japan, attacked Pearl Harbor and brought the USA also into the war on our side.

Hitler, with many of his Army divisions immobilized by the snow and frost of 'General Winter' on the *Ostfront* in Russia, began to worry that Britain and America would seize the opportunity to start a Second Front in the West. He was convinced that the Allied forces would re-enter Europe through Norway. The capital ships of his High Seas Fleet — the pocket battleships *Scharnhorst* and *Gneisenau* and the cruiser *Prinz Eugen* — were bottled up in the port of Brest in North-west France. He determined that, in the next spell of bad weather, they should slip through the Channel and proceed to Norway where their considerable firepower could be decisive in the event of an attempted Allied landing.

A German fighter pilot, veteran of the *Blitzkrieg* against Russia, tells in his diary of the Channel dash as it affected him. To help protect the Fleet his squadron of Messerschmitt 109s had been moved to an airfield near the Dutch coast.

HEINZ KNOKE

10.16 hours; alert for action!

It does not take long for the flight to clear the snow-covered airfield.

Out to sea, the Fleet is under heavy attacks by the Tommies. Yesterday they sent into action the last of their remaining Swordfish. The British crews must have known that they would never return.

We are to intercept a formation of attacking Blenheims. Visibility is still very poor. Our eyes try to penetrate the fog. The sea below is rough. Minesweepers come into view. The flight commander fires off the recognition flare signals. The ships are instructed to open fire on any approaching aircraft.

My aircraft is buffeted by sudden gusts of wind. It skims only a few feet above the white crests of the ominously surging green waves.

Calls from base constantly report the enemy's positions. The farther we go out to sea, the worse the radio reception becomes. It is fifteen minutes since we were airborne. According to reports from base, we may expect at any moment to encounter our Blenheims.

I adjust the reflector sights and set my guns ready to fire. Suddenly I observe some shadows in the fog to our left.

There they are!

We all pull round at once. Everyone wants to get in the first shot. Sergeant Wolf, my wingman for the past six months, draws alongside. He nods his head, and I clearly see the white of his teeth through the plexiglass window as he grins broadly.

There are twelve Blenheims. There are twelve of us also. One for each. A Blenheim ahead is in my sights and I am ready to fire before he spots me. The Tommy pulls his aircraft up sharply, trying to dodge into the overcast.

I follow him round and keep my sights upon him. Fire! I press both buttons on my stick. I watch my tracers go into his left wing at a range of 150 feet, and then into the left side of the fuselage. We both bank steeply to the left. I keep my thumb pressing on the firing-button. His left engine is hit. Wisps of cloud obscure my view. The Tommy vanishes into the overcast.

Woomf!

The cockpit is full of flying splinters. Just over my right shoulder there is a large gaping hole. I also notice that two shell-holes have appeared in my left wing.

There is the Blenheim again, just ahead. Once again I open fire. And then I am in the clouds.

The Tommy in front of me dissolves into a great shadow.

I now notice that my canopy has worked loose. I also smell burning. I gently throttle back and ease the stick forwards. A few seconds later the sea is again visible.

What if my plane is on fire?

I cautiously turn round. The canopy mounting behind me on the right has been torn away, and the plexiglass window in the rear of the fuselage is missing. By this time my Tommy is no longer in view.

Still the smell of burning persists. Blast it! What the hell can the matter be? My engine still runs smoothly: revs seem to be normal. According to the instruments there is nothing wrong. So what can be burning?

The Blenheim has been severly hit; but with a little luck it should reach the coast of England again about the time I go down in flames into the sea. A fine thing!

I make a wide turn to the left. On a course of 100, according to my calculations. I am bound to reach the coast of Holland somewhere. There is nothing to be seen of the others. I try calling them by radio, but get no reply.

Minutes drag on interminably. The time is now 11.26 hours: seventy minutes since take-off. The smell of burning gradually diminishes; but the canopy becomes increasingly loose. Surely I ought to have sighted land by now; if only I had some idea of my position! I have no faith in my compass. But then there is always the possibility that it may be right, nevertheless.

In another ten minutes I shall be compelled to land. The needle of the fuel-gauge indicator points to zero.

Land in sight! But then I suddenly find myself over water again, although I have not altered course. Is that blasted compass really working, or not? There is no sense in changing course now; so I just fly obstinately as before.

Once again land looms ahead. The flat countryside is dotted by a number of lakes behind dykes. I finally get my bearings. I am over the north of Holland.

Two minutes later I come down to land on one of the

long concrete runways at Leuwarden. Outside the control tower the soldiers come crowding round my plane. It looks very much the worse for wear. When I try to push the canopy open it drops off altogether and falls on to the wing. Behind my head, part of the fuselage has been shot away. Along the right side there are several jagged holes. The metal is charred and black. So that was what I had smelled burning.

Knoke was right about the fate of the Swordfish and their Fleet Air Arm crews.

The High Seas Fleet had sailed from Brest shortly before midnight on February 11th, immediately upon the All Clear after a routine raid by RAF Wellington bombers. The weather was as bad as Hitler required – strong winds, snowstorms, and poor visibility. At maximum speed, twenty-seven knots, the capital ships and their escorting destroyers and E-boats pushed on up the Channel. They kept as close as possible to the French coast and maintained strict radio silence. Even the *Luftwaffe* staff officer responsible for the Fleet's fighter cover could follow its progress only from coastal radar reports.

Because of the weather, and a series of mishaps, RAF patrols did not sight the enemy fleet until it was off Le Touquet and fast approaching the Straits of Dover. In the narrow Straits it would be nearer to England than at any other moment of the voyage. By another series of mishaps there were no bombers at readiness in the south-east of England, and no Naval vessels larger than motor torpedo-boats available. The only torpedo-bombers stationed within range of the Straits were seven RAF Beauforts at Thorney Island in Hampshire and six near-obsolete 90-mph Fleet Air Arm Swordfish biplanes at Manston in Kent.

The Swordfish squadron, under the command of Lieutenant-Commander Eugene Esmonde, an experienced pilot who had already led a daring torpedo attack on the battleship *Bismarck*, was detailed to make the first attack. The time was 11.25. The range of the Swordfish was short; in order to make contact they would have to take off within the hour.

Five squadrons of RAF Spitfires were detailed to escort the Naval planes, to deal with the German fighters while the torpedo-bombers went for the ships. Only one squadron was able to reach Manston in time.

At 12.28, three minutes late, the six Swordfish escorted by only ten Spitfires set out to engage the mighty High Seas Fleet as it passed through the Straits of Dover.

Within fifteen minutes they sighted the enemy force. At the same instant the patrolling formations of F-W 90s and Me 109s made for them.

The battle began. The Swordfish, in two flights of three, pressed on towards their target – grey-painted battleships scarcely visible against the heaving grey of the Channel in the thick murk of a grey winter's day. The Spitfires fought desperately to protect their charges, but there were too many German fighters. The Swordfish were already riddled by machine-gun bullets and cannon shells when they reached the barrage of flak put up by the Fleet.

Every ship hurled salvo after salvo of fire at the on-coming biplanes. The port wing was torn off Esmonde's already damaged Swordfish, and he crashed into the sea. The two planes remaining in his flight managed to release their torpedoes, but by now the encircling destroyers had hidden the battleships behind a thick smokescreen and the

The Swordfish pressed on towards their target

torpedo-gunners' aim was wild. Torpedoes gone, these two Swordfish were also brought down. The second flight of three disappeared into the smokescreen and inferno of bursting shells, and was never seen again.

All six Swordfish were lost. Five Naval airmen, from the first flight, were rescued from the sea by British MTBs. The other thirteen died. None of the torpedoes found its mark.

Subsequent torpedo and bomber attacks by RAF planes were equally unsuccessful, nor did the Royal Navy's small surface vessels score any hits. Undamaged (except superficially, by mines) the High Seas Fleet reached the mouth of the Elbe, and safety.

Lieutenant-Commander Esmonde was posthumously awarded the first Fleet Air Arm V C.

CHAPTER EIGHT

Kill The Admiral!

In war the men responsible – the politicians and the generals – seldom run the everyday risks of the fighting men. There have been some exceptions. In the Second World War six high-ranking British officers were captured, and imprisoned in Italy. Two British Guards officers, with the help of Cretan guerrillas, kidnapped and whisked away to Cairo the local Nazi general. Commandos tried to kill or capture Rommel in his desert headquarters on the coast of North Africa.

Unfortunately Rommel was not there at the time and the mission failed. One that succeeded brilliantly was a USAF attack on a Japanese admiral.

Admiral Isoroku Yamamoto was the master mind behind the Japanese raid on Pearl Harbor which brought the United States into the war. As such he was Public Enemy No 1.

By patient work American experts managed to break the Japanese Naval code. Intercepting a signal from Rabaul in the Pacific, Washington learned that Yamamoto, flying in one of two 'Betty' bombers escorted by six Zero fighters, would touch down at Ballale airstrip south of Bougainville at 09.45 on Sunday April 18th, 1943. Immediately the USAF at Henderson airfield, Guadalcanal, was instructed to intercept and shoot him down.

Henderson received the order during the evening of the

17th. Overnight eighteen P-38 Lightnings drawn from the 339th, 12th and 70th Fighter Squadrons were fitted with extra fuel tanks flown in from a distant bomber base. At 07.25 on the morning of the 18th, under the command of Major John Mitchell, they took off for a point north-west of Ballale. Mitchell, with thirteen others, was to engage the admiral's escorting Zeros while Captain Thomas Lanphier and his wingman Lieutenant Rex Barber, backed by Lieutenants McLanahan and Moore, were to shoot down the Betty bombers – and kill the admiral.

McLanahan blew a tyre on take-off, and within minutes Moore had to turn back because of a blocked fuel feed. Mitchell detached two of his thirteen Lightnings, piloted by Lieutenants Holmes and Hine, to back up Lanphier and Barber.

The morning was clear and sunny with little wind. To avoid detection by coastal shipping, patrolling fighters from the enemy air base at Kahili, and radar, the sixteen remaining P-38s took a circuitous route round Japanese-held islands, and flew at only fifty feet above the sea.

At exactly the right time they reached the patch of sky where they hoped to intercept the admiral's flight.

THOMAS LANPHIER

I discerned some black specks several thousand feet above us and about five miles away which looked like bursts of anti-aircraft.

Focusing more intently, I gradually determined that what I saw were two enemy bombers escorted by six Zeros. Just as the cablegram from Washington had promised, here came Isoroku Yamamoto and his gang, accompanied by exactly six Zeros, at 09.35 on the morning of April 18th, 1943.

Without taking my eyes from the Jap formation I switched to my internal fuel tanks and dropped my belly tanks, so that I could move with agility and speed. I had no need to look for Barber; I knew from experience that he would be glued beside me.

I turned right and began to climb parallel to the course of the enemy formation, keeping as much speed as my wide-open engines would give me in order to stay in front of my quarry. Our tactical situation was by no means encouraging. Rather than being, as planned, at 10,000 feet waiting for the Jap in the position where altitude could be converted to a fast dive out of the sun, my section had been caught, by a scant few seconds, in the least desirable of all tactical positions in aerial combat. We were below and in front of the enemy and had only four aircraft to his eight.

Mitchell, too, had to scramble for his assigned post at 20,000 feet. As I angled across in front of the target, straining to reach at least the same altitude as the admiral's formation before being detected, Mitchell led his covering pilots in their rocketing climb for altitude, expecting at any moment to run into some of the Jap fighters from Kahili.

Salt must have flavoured the air for us that day for neither Mitchell's nor my section were discovered by the Japs for a precious two minutes after we saw them. Although, during these two minutes, I did lose Holmes and Hine, when Holmes called out that he could not release his wing tanks, and levelling off, went on down the coast kicking and slewing his ship in an effort to tear them off. Hine, as was his job as wingman, stayed with him.

Just at the moment Barber and I reached Yamamoto's

approximate altitude at a point some two miles to his right and about a mile in front of him, his Zero cover spotted us. They must have yelled a warning over the radio because, a second after, their belly tanks began to drop away from them (a sure sign they had seen us and were clearing for action) and they nosed over in a concerted dive to head us off, the leading bomber executed a violent wing over and dived away from us towards the left, heading back the way he had come. Simultaneously, the bomber flying beside him veered over towards Barber and me.

By this time we were closing in fast on the latter bomber, but the three Zeros who had been flying on the seaward side of the formation were pelting down between it and us at a rate which apparently would bring them to us before we got to the bomber. A short distance behind them were coming the three Zeros from the inland side of the formation. Holmes and Hine were off down the beach, out of sight, and Mitchell and his boys were also out of sight, climbing towards what they had every reason to believe would be the biggest fight of all. Barber and I were left free to have at anything in sight in accomplishing our objective.

The next couple of minutes developed into quite a brawl. Fearing we would never get to the bomber before the Zeros got to us, I horsed back on my wheel to bring my guns to bear on the lead Zero diving down upon me. Buck fever started me firing long before I had the nose of my Lightning pointed in his direction . . . I wasted a lot of ammunition getting on him but, just as I got squared away at him and had time for the fleeting thought that we were going to collide head-on, the stream of steel from my four machine guns and my cannon ripped one of his wings away. He twisted under me streaming flame and smoke.

His two wingmen were so close behind and to either side of him that I shot between them with no shots traded. Even so, they hurtled by so savagely that I was reminded that I had better get my job done and get out before I got hurt by what were obviously maddened Japanese in those Zeros.

At that moment, heading almost straight up into the blue sky, I kicked my ship over on its back and looked below me for the lead bomber that had dived inland when we were first sighted. As I hung there I got an impression, off to the east, of a swirl of aircraft against the sky. One Lightning silhouetted against the light amid several Zeros. That was Barber, having his own troubles.

The excitement of a fight must work wonders for a man's vision, for at the same time that I saw Barber working out with the Japs on my right, and glimpsed the two Zeros I had just overshot wheeling around to come back at me from that same general direction, I spotted a shadow moving across the treetops below. I focused on it and found it to be the elusive bomber I was seeking. It was skimming along the surface of the jungle heading once again for Kahili. The pilot must have executed a complete circle in his evasive dive and flattened out of it, once again on his original course.

I pointed my nose down and squared away in a dive towards him. His original leading position, and his frantic efforts to elude me, assured me he carried what we had come a long way to destroy. He was moving directly across my line of flight from my left as I, too, flattened out on the treetops and prepared to slide up beside him for a point-blank shot. As I moved in on him I began to realize that I had picked up too much speed in my dive and was going to overshoot him unless I slowed down. For the first time since we had sighted the Jap formation, I cut back on my throttles. Crossing my controls, I went into a skid to further brake my speed.

I pointed my nose down and squared away in a dive towards him

As I did so, the two Zeros I had not spoken to as we passed by upstairs, showed up again. They, too, were diving towards the bomber from an angle slightly off to my right. Their intent was obviously to try and get me before I got the bomber; the two Zeros and I were going to arrive at the same place at the same time.

We very nearly did. The next three or four seconds became a life and death problem in time and distance. I remember feeling very stubborn just then, about making the most of that one good shot I had coming up at that bomber, no matter what the high-priced talent in the two Zeros wanted to make of it.

I applied myself to my gunnery and, taking no chances of missing, began firing a long steady burst across the bomber's line of flight from approximately right angles. Long before I considered myself in range, the bomber's right engine, and then his right wing, began to burn. I had accomplished my part of the mission. Once afire, no Jap aircraft ever ceased burning, short of blowing up. And all on board were too close to earth to jump for their lives. The two onrushing Zeros shot by just then, apparently unwilling to chance a crash in the jungle in order to get me.

At the same instant as they swooped across the top of my canopy, I was in trouble from another source. Out of the bomber's tail was puffing a steady series of shots from the cannon lodged back there. My belly already scraping the trees, I could not duck under it. And I hesitated to pull up over its line of fire since I was already going so slow that I would be left hanging in mid-air in a sitting-duck position, near stalling speed – and the bothersome pair of Zeros were undoubtedly scurrying around into position for another pass at me.

Apparently the only numbers up for liquidation that day were all Japanese, however, for just as I moved into range of its cannon, the bomber's right wing came off and it plunged into the jungle and exploded.

Mission completed: the admiral was dead.

This great air battle was only one of many fought in the Far East theatre of war, but the killing of their commander-in-chief – following soon after their defeat in the Battle of Midway – was a shattering blow to the morale of the officers of the Imperial Japanese Navy.

CHAPTER NINE

The Master Bombers

The fighter pilot soaring into the clear blue sky is the knight in shining armour who rides forth from the castle to challenge his peers among the besieging armies beyond the moat. When he kills, he kills a warrior like himself, never a woman or child. If victorious he becomes an ace – though this title was discouraged in the Second World War. The Air Ministry felt it undesirable so to glamorize the fighter pilots when the whole Service was fighting as courageously. Official policy, however, does not change human nature, and the names of such men as 'Johnnie' Johnson, 'Sailor' Malan, 'Paddy' Finucane, 'Screwball' Beurling, Stanford Tuck, 'Ginger' Lacey and many others were soon widely known.

Bomber crews needed courage of a different kind. Sometimes at dusk, sometimes at midnight, sometimes in the early hours of the morning, they took off in their heavily laden, clumsy, slow aircraft to carry the war into enemy territory. Often they flew for ten hours or more; often they were not back by dawn. Often, all too often, they did not come back at all.

Operations were cancelled if the 'met' report was a bad one. But a good 'met' report was no guarantee that the weather would not turn filthy en route. The bombers were caught out in gales, in blizzards, in violent electric storms, in fog. The aircraft were neither comfortable nor weatherproof – rain poured through the windscreen, instruments iced up – yet the crews preferred bad weather to good. If the night was bright moonlight and perfect for flying it was perfect, too, for the enemy's night fighters, searchlights, and flak.

The flak was the worst of it.

At the height they were flying the bomber crews would, unless they were in the first wave, see the target from miles off. The novice thought it beautiful: the white criss-crossing beams of the searchlights; the smaller guns' tracer – red, yellow, green – which seemed to climb slowly at first and to gather speed as it came closer; the silver star-shaped bursts of the high-explosive shells hurled up by the heavies; and below the aerial fireworks, against the blackness of the ground, the sparkling trails of incendiary bombs and the great blooming roses of established fires.

The novice made friends among the other crews in his squadron. On the night when he saw one of their aircraft burst into flames and dive twisting into the deck, the scene over the target lost its beauty and became evil. Then his own aircraft was hit. This time it limped home, but now he himself had smelled the cordite and heard the white-hot fragments tear through the flimsy fabric of the fuselage. He had seen the blood streaming down the flight engineer's face. Now he knew that it could happen to him.

The air-gunners could sometimes scare off, hit, or even shoot down an attacking night fighter, or the pilot could lose him in cloud. Neither firepower nor skill were any use against radar-controlled flak. Over the target area, where the flak was thickest, the aircraft had to be held rock-steady so that the bomb-aimer could drop his bombs.

Germany is a big country and the North Sea is wide. If your bomber was hit over the target area you were a long way from home. If it was so badly damaged that you could not make it, the best you could hope for was a safe parachute drop and a German prison camp. If you had to ditch in the North Sea, and did not drown, you were lucky if your rubber dinghy was sighted even by a German patrol.

You were often airsick. You could not move easily about the aircraft in your bulky flying suit – anyway to move would mean unplugging the oxygen supply, the heating wires, and the intercom. It would also upset the bomber's trim. You could not speak to the rest of the crew except over the inter-com, one at a time; and the static and the roar of the engines made it difficult to hear what the other chap was saying.

Even when it had gone well, when you had found the right target, dropped your bombs squarely in the middle of it and flown out unscathed, you did not have the fighter pilot's joy in victory. You had bombed a city; you knew that you must have killed old people, women, and children.

The noise of the engines, and the fumes which gathered in the cabin, had a deadening effect. All that you felt able to do was endure. You sat in your cramped seat, looking forward to the moment of touch-down, bacon and eggs for breakfast, and bed.

Because the bomber crews were under this tremendous strain, the limit of a 'tour' was fifty operations.

Wing Commander Guy Gibson DSO, DFC, had completed two bombing tours and a spell as a night fighter pilot when he was posted to Group Headquarters 'to help write a book for would-be bomber pilots'. Then a Boffin,

'Jeff', Barnes Wallis of Vickers, came up with a new weapon and a plan for its use.

The chief industrial area of Germany was the Ruhr Valley whose vast coalfields, steelworks, and armament factories were vital to the war effort. It was hotly defended and none of us liked going there, so we called it 'Happy Valley'. The Ruhr got its water supply from one mighty dam, the Möhne, and its hydro-electric power from another, the Eder. The Möhne Dam was the more important. There, 140 million tons of water were held in check by concrete barrages 140 feet thick, impervious to normal bombing.

What Wallis had invented was a giant mine which *if dropped on the right spot at the right time from an aircraft flying at the right height and speed* would explode forty feet under water against the barrage wall and topple it, releasing all those millions of tons of water into the valley below.

The job could only be done when the dam was full, ie, the level of the water four feet from the top of the wall. This was estimated to be in six weeks' time, which meant that the mine-carrying bombers would have to operate in moonlight. They would have to fly low all the way and drop their bombs from a height of sixty feet – which meant that the crews had no hope of baling out.

Guy Gibson was chosen to lead the raid. In those six weeks he had to get together and train for this unusual operation a squadron of crack pilots, navigators, wireless operators, bomb-aimers, flight-engineers, and air-gunners. He had to indent for all the necessary, sometimes special equipment. In view of the urgency and magnitude of the operation his requirements were given Air Ministry approval in advance, and top priority; but it was a formidable task. The greatest secrecy had to be maintained or the Germans would have mustered enough ground defences and night fighters to make the raid impossible. Even the crews could not be told the target. Flying in aircraft with windows tinted to simulate night-flying conditions, they were trained in pinpoint navigation, in following canals and rivers, in flying low over water. It proved impossible to judge their own height to the exact limits necessary, and there was a great danger of ditching. Another Boffin solved the problem — two spotlights so directed that from the right height their beams would meet and merge on the surface of the water below. This was fine for telling the pilot he was at the specified height over the reservoir; it was also another bonus for the enemy defences, which would now have targets with lights on!

Six weeks after the 'flap' began, all was ready. On May 16th, 1943, photo-reconnaissance aircraft reported that the water level was the required four feet below the top of the barrage. Nineteen brand-new highly tuned Lancasters (minus the upper gunner's turret to part compensate for the extra load) were armed with their giant mines. The crews were briefed. No other bombers were to operate that night. The air officer commanding 5 Group made a special journey to Scampton to wish them luck.

617 Squadron, the Master Bombers, took off.

On the way out, one Lancaster hit the North Sea and bounced off, losing its mine and damaging its two outboard engines; it got home on the inboard two. A second was hit by flak over Holland and also had to return. Over the Ruhr the pilot of a third, momentarily blinded by searchlights, lost control; his aircraft reared up, plunged down, burst into flames, and exploded.

The remaining sixteen Lancasters flew on, so low that

the moon cast their gigantic moving shadows across the German countryside.

GUY GIBSON

As we came over the hill, we saw the Möhne Lake. Then we saw the dam itself. In that light it looked squat and heavy and unconquerable; it looked grey and solid in the moonlight, as though it were part of the countryside itself and just as immovable. A structure like a battleship was showering out flak all along its length, but some came from the powerhouse below it and nearby. There were no searchlights. It was light flak, mostly green, yellow, and red, and the colours of the tracer reflected upon the face of the water in the lake. The reflections on the dead calm of the black water made it seem there was twice as much as there really was.

'Did you say these gunners were out of practice?' asked Spam, sarcastically.

'They certainly seem awake now,' said Terry.

They were awake all right. No matter what people say, the Germans certainly have a good warning system. I scowled to myself as I remembered telling the boys an hour or so ago that they would probably only be the German equivalent of the Home Guard and in bed by the time we arrived.

It was hard to say exactly how many guns there were, but tracers seemed to be coming from about five positions, probably making twelve guns in all. It was hard at first to tell the calibre of the shells, but after one of the boys had been hit, we were informed over the RT that they were either 20-mm type or 37-mm, which, as everyone knows, are nasty little things.

We circled around stealthily, picking up the various landmarks upon which we had planned our method of attack, making use of some and avoiding others; every time we came within range of those bloody-minded flak-gunners they let us have it.

Down below, the Möhne Lake was silent and black and deep, and I spoke to my crew.

'Well, boys, I suppose we had better start the ball rolling.' This with no enthusiasm whatsoever. 'Hello, all Cooler aircraft. I am going to attack. Stand by to come in to attack in your order when I tell you.'

Then to Hoppy: 'Hello, "M Mother". Stand by to take over if anything happens.'

Hoppy's clear and casual voice came back. 'OK, leader. Good luck.'

Then the boys dispersed to the prearranged hiding-spots in the hills, so that they should not be seen either from the ground or from the air, and we began to get into position for our approach. We circled wide and came around down moon, over the high hills at the eastern end of the lake. On straightening up we began to dive towards the flat, ominous water two miles away. Over the front turret was the dam silhouetted against the haze of the Ruhr Valley. We could see the towers. We could see the sluices. We could see everything. Spam, the bomb-aimer, said 'Good show. This is wizard.' He had been a bit worried, as all bomb-aimers are, in case they cannot see their aiming points, but as we came in over the tall fir trees his voice came up again rather quickly. 'You're going to hit them. You're going to hit those trees.'

'That's all right, Spam. I'm just getting my height.'

To Terry: 'Check height, Terry.'

To Pulford: 'Speed control, Flight-Engineer.'

To Trevor: 'All guns ready, gunners.'

To Spam: 'Coming up, Spam.'

Terry turned on the spotlights and began giving directions – 'Down – down – down. Steady – steady.' We were then exactly sixty feet.

Pulford began working the speed: first he put on a little flap to slow us down, then he opened the throttles to get the air-speed indicator exactly against the red mark. Spam began lining up his sights against the towers. He had turned the fusing switch to the 'ON' position. I began flying.

The gunners had seen us coming. They could see us coming with our spotlights on for over two miles away. Now they opened up and the tracers began swirling towards us; some were even bouncing off the smooth surface of the lake. This was a horrible moment: we were being dragged along at four miles a minute, almost against our will, towards the things we were going to destroy. I think at that moment the boys did not want to go. I know I did not want to go. I thought to myself, 'In another minute we shall all be dead – so what?' I thought again, 'This is terrible – this feeling of fear – if it is fear.' By now we were a few hundred yards away, and I said quickly to Pulford, under my breath, 'Better leave the throttles open now and stand by to pull me out of the seat if I get hit.' As I glanced at him I thought he looked a little glum on hearing this.

The Lancaster was really moving and I began looking through the special sight on my windscreen. Spam had his eyes glued to the bomb-sight in front, his hand on his button; a special mechanism on board had already begun to work so that the mine would drop (we hoped) in the right spot. Terry was still checking the height. Joe and Trev began to raise their guns. The flak could see us quite clearly now. It was not exactly inferno. I have been through far worse flak fire than that; but we were very low. There was something sinister and slightly unnerving about the whole operation. My aircraft was so small and the dam was so large; it was thick and solid, and now it was angry. My aircraft was very small. We skimmed along the surface of the lake, and as we went my gunner was firing into the defences, and the defences were firing back with vigour, their shells whistling past us. For some reason, we were not being hit.

Spam said, 'Left – little more left – steady – steady – steady – coming up.' Of the next few seconds I remember only a series of kaleidoscopic incidents.

The chatter from Joe's front guns pushing out tracers which bounced off the left-hand flak tower.

Pulford crouching beside me.

The smell of burnt cordite.

The cold sweat underneath my oxygen mask.

The tracers flashing past the windows – they all seemed the same colour now – and the inaccuracy of the gun positions near the power-station; they were firing in the wrong direction.

The closeness of the dam wall.

Spam's exultant, 'Mine gone.'

Hutch's red Very lights to blind the flak-gunners.

The speed of the whole thing.

Someone saying over the RT, 'Good show, leader. Nice work.'

Then it was all over, and at last we were out of range, and there came over us all, I think, an immense feeling of relief and confidence.

Trevor said, 'I will get those gunners,' and he began to spray the dam with bullets until at last he, too, was out of range. As we circled round we could see a great 1,000-feet column of whiteness still hanging in the air where our

mine had exploded. We could see with satisfaction that
Spam had been good, and it had gone off in the right
position. Then, as we came closer, we could see that the
explosion of the mine had caused a great disturbance
upon the surface of the lake and the water had become
broken and furious, as though it were being lashed by a
gale. At first we thought that the dam itself had broken,
because great sheets of water were slopping over the top
of the wall like a gigantic basin. This caused some delay,
because our mines could only be dropped in calm water,
and we would have to wait until all became still again.

We waited.

We waited about ten minutes, but it seemed hours to
us. It must have seemed even longer to Hoppy, who was
the next to attack. Meanwhile, all the fighters had now
collected over our target. They knew our game by now,
but we were flying too low for them; they could not see
us and there were no attacks.

At last – 'Hello, "M Mother". You may attack now.
Good luck.'

'OK. Attacking.'

Hoppy, the Englishman, casual, but very efficient, keen
now on only one thing, which was war. He began his
attack.

He began going down over the trees where I had come
from a few moments before. We could see his spotlights
quite clearly, slowly closing together as he ran across the
water. We saw him approach. The flak, by now, had got
an idea from which direction the attack was coming, and
they let him have it. When he was about 100 yards away
someone said, hoarsely, over the RT: 'Hell! he has been
hit.'

'M Mother' was on fire: an unlucky shot had got him in
one of the inboard petrol tanks and a long jet of flame

was beginning to stream out. I saw him drop his mine, but his bomb-aimer must have been wounded, because it fell straight on to the powerhouse on the other side of the dam. But Hoppy staggered on, trying to gain altitude so that his crew could bale out. When he had got up to about 500 feet there was a vivid flash in the sky and one wing fell off; his aircraft disintegrated and fell to the ground in cascading, flaming fragments. There it began to burn quite gently and rather sinisterly in a field some three miles beyond the dam.

Someone said, 'Poor old Hoppy!'

Another said, 'We'll get 'em for this.'

A furious rage surged up inside my own crew, and Trevor said, 'Let's go in and murder those gunners.' As he spoke, Hoppy's mine went up. It went up behind the powerhouse with a tremendous yellow explosion and left in the air a great ball of black smoke; again there was a long wait while we watched for this to clear. There was so little wind that it took a long time.

Many minutes later I told Mickey to attack; he seemed quite confident, and we ran in beside him and a little in front; as we turned, Trevor did his best to get those gunners as he had promised.

Bob Hay, Mickey's bomb-aimer, did a good job, and his mine dropped in exactly the right place. There was again a gigantic explosion as the whole surface of the lake shook, then spewed forth its cascade of white water. Mickey was all right; he got through. But he had been hit several times and one wing tank lost all its petrol. I could see the vicious tracer from his rear-gunner giving one gun position a hail of bullets as he swept over. Then he called up, 'OK. Attack completed.' It was then that I thought that the dam wall had moved. Of course we could not see anything, but if Jeff's theory had been correct, it should

his mine dropped in smoke he picked . . .

have cracked by now. If only we could go on pushing it by dropping more successful mines, it would surely move back on its axis and collapse.

Once again we watched for the water to calm down. Then in came Melvyn Young in 'D Dog'. I yelled to him, 'Be careful of the flak. It's pretty hot.'

He said, 'OK.'

I yelled again, 'Trevor's going to beat them up on the other side. He'll take most of it off you.'

Melvyn's voice again. 'OK. Thanks.' And so as D Dog ran in we stayed at a fairly safe distance on the other side, firing with all guns at the defences, and the defences, like the stooges they were, firing back at us. We were both out of range of each other, but the ruse seemed to work, and we flicked on our identification lights to let them see us even more clearly. Melvyn's mine went in, again in exactly the right spot, and this time a colossal wall of water swept right over the dam and kept on going. Melvyn said, 'I think I've done it. I've broken it.' But we were in a better position to see than he, and it had not rolled down yet. We were all getting pretty excited by now, and I screamed like a schoolboy over the RT: 'Wizard show, Melvyn. I think it'll go on the next one.'

When at last the water had all subsided I called up Nº 5 – David Maltby – and told him to attack. He came in fast, and I saw his mine fall within feet of the right spot; once again the flak, the explosion and wall of water. But this time we were on the wrong side of the wall and could see what had happened. We watched for about five minutes, and it was rather hard to see anything, for by now the air was full of spray from these explosions, which had settled like mist on our windscreens. Time was getting short, so I called up Dave Shannon and told him to come in.

As he turned I got close to the dam wall and then saw what had happened. It had rolled over, but I could not believe my eyes. I heard someone shout, 'I think she has gone! I think she has gone!' Other voices took up the cry and quickly I said, 'Stand by until I make a recco.' I remembered that Dave was going in to attack and told him to turn away and not to approach the target. We had a closer look. Now there was no doubt about it; there was a great breach 100 yards across, and the water, looking like stirred porridge in the moonlight, was gushing out and rolling into the Ruhr Valley towards the industrial centres of Germany's Third Reich.

Nearly all the flak had now stopped, and the other boys came down from the hills to have a closer look to see what had been done. There was no doubt about it at all – the Möhne Dam had been breached and the gunners on top of the dam, except for one man, had all run for their lives towards the safety of solid ground: this remaining gunner was a brave man, but one of the boys quickly extinguished his flak with a burst of well-aimed tracer. Now it was all quiet, except for the roar of the water which steamed and hissed its way from its 150-foot head. Then we began to shout and scream and act like madmen over the RT, for this was a tremendous sight, a sight which probably no man will ever see again.

Quickly I told Hutch to tap out the message, 'Nigger', to my station, and when this was handed to the air officer commanding there was (I heard afterwards) great excitement in the operations room. The scientist jumped up and danced round the room.

Then I looked again at the dam and at the water, while all around me the boys were doing the same. It was the most amazing sight. The whole valley was beginning to fill with fog from the steam of the gushing water, and down in the foggy valley we saw cars speeding along the roads in front of this great wave of water, which was chasing them and going faster than they could ever hope to go. I saw their headlights burning and I saw water overtake them, wave by wave, and then the colour of the headlights underneath the water changing from light blue to green, from green to dark purple, until there was no longer anything except the water bouncing down in great waves. The floods raced on, carrying with them as they went -- viaducts, railways, bridges, and everything that stood in their path. Three miles beyond the dam the remains of Hoppy's aircraft were still burning gently, a dull red glow on the ground.

The main force of Lancasters went on to the Eder and repeated the performance, while a sub-flight demolished a third, smaller, dam at Sorpe.

Of the nineteen Lancasters which set out that night, eight aircraft – fifty-four men – did not return.

Guy Gibson, who was awarded the Victoria Cross for this operation, was killed on a later one.

CHAPTER TEN

Festung Europa

When Hitler realized that the Allies would soon invade *Festung Europa* – the stronghold of Europe – he put into effect a Plan for the defence of the *Reich*.

Part of the Plan was to build, well back from the German frontiers, a large number of secondary aerodromes and even airstrips from which the *Luftwaffe* could operate when their main forward bases were destroyed. He had so many of these aerodromes and airfields built that the squadrons, preceded by their own mobile flak battalions and ground personnel, could move from one to another speedily as the need arose. Such an airfield was called an *Einsatz* – a field to be used as a substitute.

It was a brilliant idea and, efficiently executed, did much to slow down the Allied Armies when they opened the Second Front in June 1944. Even when the Allied Air Forces were able to use air bases in Germany itself, the *Luftwaffe*, operating from a different *Einsatz* every few days, inflicted such heavy losses among the troops that Army HQ appealed to the RAF to destroy more of the *Luftwaffe* on the ground.

The difficulty was to know which airfields the Germans were using at any given moment, and to get there before they dispersed their machines.

Tempests of (122) Fighter Wing, led by Wing Commander Pierre Clostermann DSO, DFC, a Frenchman

from Alsace, were held in immediate readiness to attack
any active enemy airfield reported to them by (49) Canadian Reconnaissance Wing. A squadron of rocket Typhoons was to make the Tempests' task easier by going in
first to silence the enemy flak.

Pierre Clostermann, like Guy Gibson, had already done
more fighting than could be reasonably expected of him.
He had recently converted to Tempests from Spitfires in
which he had been operating almost continuously
since 1941. By now, April 1945, he had made more
than 400 sorties – dogfights in the skies over Britain,
escort for USAF Liberators and Flying Fortresses on
their mass daylight raids into Germany, strafes on shipping and flying-bomb sites, fighter cover for the invading
Allied Armies.

No man could keep this up for ever. The constant fight
to conquer fear is very tiring. Each sortie becomes a
greater effort than the one before. This vivid account of a
low-level attack on an *Einsatz* aerodrome conveys the
reactions of a man who has fought too well for too
long.

(49) Reconnaissance Squadron have just telephoned to
report that one of their planes has seen forty Messerschmitts and fifteen Arado two-seaters land at Schwerin.

'GCC' is Group Central Control, 'Kenway' is the
controller, 'Spy' is the nickname of the wing intelligence
officer, and 'Filmstar' is the codename of the Tempest
formation.

PIERRE CLOSTERMANN

Schwerin, a fine big airfield by a lake, west of the town of the same name. I put up a rapid sketch on the blackboard the three runways forming a triangle, the probable location of the aircraft, from 49 Wing report.

The Jerries had landed at 11.40 hours. It was now 12.10 hours. Refuelling and rearming the planes would take the Germans a good hour – we just had time to catch them before they flew off, dispersed or hid in the pine woods.

I gave last instructions, while Spy phoned through to GCC to tell them what we were going to do and to ask for the rocket Typhoons to be laid on.

'We shall attack from north to south, all eight together, in line abreast, with a 200-yard interval between aircraft. Speed 530-40 mph. Each pilot will pick out his target as he dives – no last-minute change of direction. Open fire at 1,000 yards and continue till point-blank range. Stay as close to the ground as you can, count up to twenty, and then break fan-wise and climb at full throttle.

'Rendezvous with the Typhoons is at 13.00 hours – late, I'm afraid, but they can't get there any earlier. The Typhoons will come down from 8,000 to 3,000 feet, thirty seconds before us and they will shoot up any flak posts they can spot with their rockets. Because there is bound to be some flak.' (Slightly forced smiles.)

'Remember that surprise, speed, and, especially, flying at zero feet, are our best defence. No point in waggling your wings and pretending you're putting off the flak boys – you'll lose a few precious mph and risk sticking a wing on the deck.

'One last bit of advice: if you are hit and have to bale out, the best way, let me remind you, is this: stick right back – jettison the hood – curl up in a ball – wait a few seconds – jerk the stick right forwards. You'll have nine chances out of ten of being thrown clear of the cockpit. Naturally I hope it won't come to that!

'Any questions? OK then, let's go!'

'Hello, Kenway, Filmstar Leader calling – what about the Tiffie boys?' I was beginning to get anxious. We had crossed the Elbe and we could already see Schwerin lake on the horizon quite clearly. No sign of the Typhoons. A few moments later Kenway answered apologetically:

'Hello, Filmstar Leader, sorry old boy, there's a cock-up about the Tiffies. Do the best you can without!'

A pleasant prospect! Without anti-flak Typhoons, we were in for the hell of a time. My voice was probably not too steady as I got my patrol into attack formation. A big blue lake edged with pine trees, cut in the middle by a peninsular on which stood the town of Schwerin, a picturesque little town with Renaissance steeples and varnished tiles, clinging to the rocks. To the west a fine airfield, intact, complete with buildings and camouflaged hangars – not many like that left in Germany.

We were at 14,000 feet and kept straight on over to the left, as if we had no intention of attacking. I took a close look at the field: the small dark crosses parked just where we had expected them showed up on the bright grass of early spring. I particularly noticed one, two, four, seven flak towers, their shadows clearly projected on the perimeter track by the sun . . .

'Look out Filmstar Leader, flak at 6 o'clock!'

Sure enough, 200 yards behind us five big black puffs from 88-mm shells had appeared. OK! Five more seconds

and then I would attack. The objective was behind us and
we were facing the sun. Fear caught me by the throat and
stopped me breathing. Aerial combat against fighters had
always found me calm – after the early stages – but flak
was different.

'Drop your babies, Filmstar.'

My stomach contracted and a wave of nausea swept
over me – the advantage of a single-seater is that you
can pass out with funk without anybody noticing.

'Quick, 180 port, go!'

This would bring us back facing the airfield, with the
sun at our backs.

'Diving full-out, Filmstar!'

My seven Tempests were beautifully echeloned on
my left although we were diving almost vertically.

'Smell of flowers,' came Bay Adams' voice mockingly
in the earphones. Flak! Christ, what flak! The entire surface of the airfield seemed to light up with flashes from
20-mm and 37-mm guns. There must have been at least
forty of them. A carpet of white puffs spread out below us
and the black puffs of the 37s stood out in regular strings
of light.

What flak! Physical fear is the most terrible thing man
can suffer – my heart leaped to my mouth, I was covered
with sweat, with sticky, clammy sweat. My clenched
toes swam in my boots.

We dived desperately into the smoke . . . explosions
and tracer to left and right crossing over and under us . . .
bangs round our wings and sinister dazzling flashes.

We were a mile from the perimeter, 150 feet from the
ground. Men were running hither and thither.

'Lower, for Christ's sake,' I yelled. The broad expanse
of grass, carved by the grey runways, tilted up before my
eyes and rushed towards me. We were doing over 450

I fired frantically, my thumb jammed on the button

mph. First a hangar ... a bowser ... then the Messerschmitts, perched clumsily on their narrow undercarts, about thirty of them, with men crouched under the wings. Too far to the left, unfortunately, outside my line of fire.

A group of a dozen Arados loomed up in my sight. I fired, I fired frantically, my thumb jammed on the button. My shells formed a ribbon of explosion worming its way between the Arados, climbing up the fuselage, hitting the engines ... smoke ... one of the planes exploded just as I was over it, and my Tempest was tossed up by the burning gust. A Tempest touched the ground and the fuselage bounded up in a shower of fragments of smashed wings and tailplanes.

More hangars in front of me. I fired a second burst – it exploded on the galvanized iron doors and the steel stanchions.

'Look out, Red 2!' My No 2 was coming straight for me, out of control, at terrific speed. His hood had gone. At 470 mph, twenty yards to my right, he went smack into a flak tower, cutting it in two underneath the platform.

The wooden frame flew into the air. A cluster of men hanging on to a gun collapsed into space. The Tempest crashed on the edge of the field, furrowing through a group of little houses, with a terrific flash of light; the engine had come adrift in a whirlwind of flames and fragments scattered in the sky.

It was all over . . . almost. One, two, three . . . the tracer bullets were pursuing me . . . I lowered my head and hunched myself up behind my rear plating . . . twelve, thirteen, fourteen . . . I was going to cheat . . . a salvo of 37 burst so close that I only got the flash of the explosions without seeing the smoke . . . splinters hailed down on my fuselage . . . nineteen, twenty! I pulled the stick back and climbed straight up into the sky. The flak kept on.

I glanced back towards Schwerin, just visible under my tailplane. A thousand feet below a Tempest was climbing in zig-zags, the tracers stubbornly pursuing him. Fires near the hangars, columns of greasy smoke, a firework display of exploding magnesium bombs. The lone Tempest caught me up, waggled his wings and formed line abreast.

'Hello, Filmstar aircraft, reform south of target, angels ten.'

'Hello, Pierre, Red 3 here. You know, I think the rest had it!'

Surely Bay couldn't be right! I scanned the 360 degrees of the horizon, and the terrific pyramid of flak bursts above Schwerin right up to the clouds, hanging in the still air. No one.

13.04 hours. We had attacked at 13.03 hours. The nightmare had lasted perhaps thirty-five seconds from the beginning of our dive and we had lost six aircraft out of eight . . .

CHAPTER ELEVEN

The Divine Wind

In the late spring of 1945 the war in Europe, against Germany, was over. The war in the Far East, against Japan, was still being fought.

The Germans had been weakened by two years of 'round-the-clock' bombing – the USAF raiding by day and the RAF by night. In some of the major cities the All-Clear never sounded. In spite of the wholesale destruction of Germany's war industries and the exhaustion of her citizens, the invading Allied Armies had to fight every inch of the way to Berlin, and lost many men.

The war against Japan was being fought mainly by the Americans who by now had regained the Pacific Islands overrun by the Japanese in '41 and '42, and had even installed themselves on outlying islands of the Japanese archipelago. In preparation to invade Japan itself the USA had built up a vast navy of Task Forces, each of which included at least one aircraft carrier. Mass formations of the fabulous B-29 Superfortresses bombed the enemy's cities to saturation point, while the Task Forces blockaded and bombarded its ports.

The *Samurai*, members of Japan's *élite* warrior caste, were dedicated to the idea of dying to defend the Emperor in battle. Now this idea was carried a stage further. Special squadrons were formed of Army and Navy airmen who would dive their bomb-laden planes straight

THE DIVINE WIND   107

into the American ships, and blow themselves up in the act. At first only obsolete or training aircraft were used on these missions; later the aircraft was a specially built flying bomb designed to be piloted by a human being and destined only to destroy itself (and its pilot) against an enemy ship.

The suicide pilots were called *Kamikaze* – 'divine wind' – because in the thirteenth century a storm had scattered and destroyed the Mongolian fleet as it sailed to invade Japan. The new *Kamikaze* were to destroy the US fleet and prevent the Americans from invading.

The idea behind the *Kamikaze* is difficult for the Western mind to accept. It worried the Allied commanders. If the Japanese ground forces fought as fanatically as the airmen, the invasion and conquest of Japan would be an even bloodier affair than that of Germany.

To end the war quickly, President Truman, Prime Minister Churchill and the Allied chiefs of staff made a decision which shocked the world. They decided to devastate Hiroshima and Nagasaki, two of Japan's most crowded cities. To do this they would use the scientists' latest and most terrible invention – the atom bomb.

Yasuo Kuwahara won the glider championship of Japan while still a schoolboy. One evening soon afterwards a captain of the Imperial Army Air Force called on his father, to enlist the boy as a recruit. Yasuo was given the chance to say *Yes* or *No*; but for a Japanese boy of fifteen, brought up to respect his father's wishes and to worship the Emperor, there was no question of refusal.

There followed months of brutally rigorous training which only the toughest survived. Yasuo managed to gain one of the coveted places in the school for fighter pilots. On his first operational sortie he brought down an

American Grumman – the first of several victories.

When the early *Kamikaze* squadrons were formed, commanding officers were reluctant to let their good men go, preferring to sacrifice the novices and the unskilled. Yasuo's successes saved him from being included. Instead, he found himself escorting the *Kamikaze* on their death flights. On one mission, the young trainee pilot chosen to die was his best friend.

Soon shortage of fuel prevented any operational flights other than the *Kamikaze* missions. Now even the best pilots were expendable.

On August 15th, 1945, Yasuo Kuwahara received his orders. Three days later he was to die as a *Kamikaze*. He was granted the usual forty-eight hours' leave to go home and say farewell to his family. The next morning he hitched a lift on an Army truck which dropped him off in a street in Hiroshima.

He was then sixteen years old.

YASUO KUWAHARA

I heard the air-raid sirens – a small concern to me, since two planes had already passed over. The lone B-29 above scarcely seemed worth considering at first. If I were only up there now in my Hayabusa, I'd rise with the sun, under his belly, and begin pumping them out from the cannons. But there wasn't a Japanese plane anywhere. The B-29 could meander at will like a grazing animal.

I kept watching him from time to time, however. There was something a little too placid about that droning. So slow, so smug. Something . . .

When I was less than half a mile from the General Headquarters a tiny speck separated from the silver belly

Hiroshima

above, and the plane moved off, picking up speed. No bigger than a marble, the speck increased to the size of a baseball. A parachute. Speculations were being made:

'What are they up to now?'

'More pamphlets?'

'Yes, more propaganda – more of the same old thing.'

All their mutterings were cut off. Suddenly a monstrous multi-coloured flashbulb went off directly in my face. Concentrated heat lightning stifled me. A blinding flicker – blue, white, and yellow. So fast it might not have really happened at all. Something inside my own head, perhaps. I sensed this last more than thought it.

I threw up my hands against the fierce flood of heat. A mighty blast furnace had opened on the world.

Then came a cataclysm which no man will ever completely describe. It was neither a roar, a boom nor a blast. It was a combination of those things with something else added – the fantastic power of earthquakes, avalanches, winds, and floods. For a moment nature had focused her wrath on the land, and the crust of the earth shuddered.

I was slammed to the earth. Darkness, pressure, choking, and the clutches of pain . . . a relief as though my body were drifting upwards. Then nothing.

Minutes, hours, even days – it was impossible to tell how long I remained unconscious. A rumbling noise overhead, perhaps a cart, seemed to awaken me. No thoughts at all at first, just a vague sensation of being alive. As my senses slowly returned, a personality began to form. Eventually it came to me. I was Corporal Yasuo Kuwahara, and I was buried alive, under a mass of debris.

My legs were pinned down but I worked an arm free enough to clear some of the litter from my face. My eyes, nose, ears, and mouth were clogged with dirt. For several minutes I choked and spat. Searing pains ran through my body, and my skin felt violently scorched.

Groaning and gasping, I opened my eyes, and it was some time before the tears cleared them enough for me to see the tiny scratch of light overhead. For a while it seemed as if I could hear people treading about, and once there came another rumbling noise. Then the sound died.

I began to writhe. 'Help! Help me!' I forced out the words with all my strength. They were like a frog's croak. Again and again I called out and then gasped in despair. The pressure was becoming unbearable.

Hours seemed to elapse. I would call, blank out, come to, call, blank out. Gradually a numbness settled and I began trying to visualize what might have happened. A big bomb. The Americans had dropped a new bomb. Was it true? While flying I had heard repeated radio warnings from the enemy in Saipan, admonishing us to surrender, stating that the greatest power the earth had ever known was soon to be unleashed on the land of the rising sun.

What an ironical situation! A suicide pilot dying on the ground, only a short distance from his home! I almost laughed! Such an ignoble way to die!

Perhaps no one would dare approach Hiroshima. Maybe all of Japan was gone. Had a B-29 circled over every city, releasing a parachute? What a thought. No more Japan! Everything gone! No, of course not, I was dreaming.

I gave a start. Dust was sifting through the hole above, and now it was a mere bird's eye peeping down at me. More dust. The eye closed. I yelled. Feeling as if my lungs might tear loose, I yelled again and again. No answer. Sobbing for air, I made my last feeble bid for help.

A few seconds later the eye blinked at me again, and transformed into a yawning mouth. 'Be patient,' a voice came. 'I'm removing the boards!' Wonderful words. Waiting as I was, the thought came that perhaps I'd been there for days. Was I completely crippled? Would I die a few moments after my release?

Sounds increased – more voices. At length the weight was lifting, darkness changing to light. 'Are you all right?' I staggered up while the whole world teetered. What a weird, swirling vision! I fell. Arms caught my body, lowering it to earth. Men in white, it seemed.

'What happened?' I croaked.

'We don't know. A new enemy weapon.'

'You'll be all right,' another said. 'Just stay here until you regain your strength. No broken bones. You'll be all right.'

They turned to go. 'Wait!' I became terrified. 'Don't go!'

'We must,' came the spectral voices. 'Hiroshima is in ruins – everyone dead or dying.'

'Don't go!' It was no use, and I broke into a painful, dry crying. But the crying itself hurt so much that I stopped and struggled for some degree of sensibility. Not until some time later did I learn that my benefactors, the men in white, were soldiers from the Army hospital who had dived under their beds when the explosion occurred, barely escaping destruction themselves. I also learned that I had been buried for nearly six hours – from 8.15 AM until 2 PM.

There was no way of determining the extent of my injuries at first, but after about thirty minutes in the open air I struggled to my feet. As I stood swaying, my vision cleared, opening a nightmarish spectacle – a horrifying sight such as I had never seen before – a sight no man must ever see again.

ACKNOWLEDGEMENTS

Both friends and strangers have helped greatly in my research by finding or loaning books, manuscripts and combat reports, and by digging into official records for some of the facts I needed. I wish to thank especially:

Frazier Dougherty, wartime fighter pilot USAF;

Paul Chevalier, ex RCN doctor, Atlantic Convoys;

Stella Hughes-Hallett, ex WRNS Flying Control Officer;

Capt A. V. Rix, DFM, ex Pathfinder pilot;

Anne Petrides, Librarian, British Embassy, Athens;

Maro Kalfa, Librarian, JUSMAGG, Athens;

Margaret McKeller, Director, US Library Service, Athens;

Rose E. B. Coombs, Head Printed Books Section, Imperial War Museum, London.

Frank S. White, Librarian, Ministry of Defence, London;

W. S. Revell, Air Historical Branch, Ministry of Defence, London;

Charles G. Worman, Historian, Air Force Museum, Ohio; and

Jane Hollowood of Pan Books.

I also wish to thank Colonel Thomas Lanphier for allowing me to reprint his account of the Yamamoto mission, and the various copyright owners who have granted permission to quote extracts from the books starred in this list of first-hand accounts of war in the air:

First World War
*Ace of Aces, René Fonck (Doubleday/Ace Books)
 Ace of the Iron Cross, Ernest Udet (Doubleday)
 Days on the Wing, Willy Coppens
 Fighting Airman, Charles Biddle (Doubleday/Ace Books)
 Flying Fury, James McCudden (Doubleday/Ace Books)
 Into the Blue, Norman Macmillan (Jarrolds)
 Knight of the Maltese Cross, Max Immelmann (Doubleday)
 The Personal Diary of Major Edward 'Mick' Mannock
*The Red Baron, Manfred von Richthofen (Doubleday/Ace Books)
*Sagittarius Rising, Cecil Lewis (Peter Davies/Corgi)
 Wind in the Wires, Duncan Grinnel-Milne (Mayflower Books)
*Winged Warfare, William Bishop (Doubleday/Ace Books)
 Winged Victory, V. M. Yeats (Cape/Sphere)
*Zeppelin, Ernest Lehmann (Longmans Green)

Second World War
*The Big Show, Pierre Clostermann (Chatto & Windus/Corgi)
 Bomber Pilot, Leonard Cheshire (Hutchinson)
 Duel of Eagles, Peter Townsend (Weidenfeld & Nicolson)
*Enemy Coast Ahead, Guy Gibson (Michael Joseph/Pan)
*Fighter Pilot, Paul Richey (Batsford/Pan)
 The First and the Last, Adolf Galland (Methuen/Fontana)
*I Flew for the Fuhrer, Heinz Knoke (Evans/Corgi)

Flight to Arras, Antoine de Saint-Exupéry (Heinemann/Penguin)

God is My Co-pilot, Robert Scott (Ballantine Books)

*Kamikaze, Yasuo Kuwahara & Gordon Allred (Ballantine Books)

*The Last Enemy, Richard Hillary (Methuen/Pan)

Lonely Warrior, Jeon Offenberg (Souvenir Press/Mayflower)

*Night Fighter, C. F. Rawnsley & Robert Wright (Collins/Corgi)

Nine Lives, Alan Deere (Hodder & Stoughton)

Samurai, Saburo Sakai (Kimber/New English Library)

Scramble!, J. R. D. Braham (Muller/Pan)

Stuka Pilot, Hans Ulrich Rudel (Ballantine Books)

Thirty Seconds over Tokyo, Ted Lawson (Random House)

Thunderbolt, Robert Johnson (Ballantine Books)

Wing Leader, J. E. Johnson (Chatto & Windus/Ballantine Books)

Most of these titles are available in bookshops or public libraries. Many other fighting airmen have published their stories but their books are, alas, out of print and unobtainable.

My only regret in compiling *Great Air Battles* is that I did not have room to quote from all of them.

If you have enjoyed this PICCOLO Book,
you may like to choose your next book
from the new PICCOLO titles listed on the
following pages.

. . . five, six seven, eight – What do you appreciate?

PICCOLO
COLOUR BOOKS

Great new titles for boys and girls from eight to twelve
Fascinating full-colour pictures on every page
Intriguing, authentic easy-to-read facts

DINOSAURS

SECRETS OF THE PAST

SCIENCE AND US

INSIDE THE EARTH

EXPLORING OTHER WORLDS

STORMS

SNAKES AND OTHER REPTILES

AIRBORNE ANIMALS

PICCOLO
COLOUR BOOKS 25p EACH

Fit your pocket – Suit your purse

The best in fun – for everyone . . .

PICCOLO
GAMES AND PUZZLES

101 BEST CARD GAMES FOR CHILDREN
NUT-CRACKERS
Puzzles and Games to boggle the mind

FUN AND GAMES OUTDOORS
JUNIOR PUZZLE BOOKS
JUNIOR CROSSWORD BOOKS
The most popular children's crosswords in Britain

BRAIN BOOSTERS
CODES AND SECRET WRITING
Piccolo – Pick of the Puzzles 20p each

PICCOLO
SUPERB STORIES – POPULAR AUTHORS

FOLYFOOT
Monica Dickens. Based on the Yorkshire Television series

FOXY
John Montgomery

FOXY AND THE BADGERS
John Montgomery. David comes to Sussex from an orphanage and finds an unusually appealing new friend . . .

THE JUNGLE BOOK
Rudyard Kipling

THE SECOND JUNGLE BOOK
Rudyard Kipling. The magic of Mowgli, child of the forest, whose adventures made him every other child's hero

TALES FROM THE HOUSE BEHIND
by the author of the world-famous Diary of Anne Frank.